T0044991

Improvised Lives

After the Postcolonial
A series sponsored by the Smuts Memorial Fund
University of Cambridge

AbdouMaliq Simone, *Improvised Lives*

Improvised Lives

*Rhythms of Endurance
in an Urban South*

AbdouMaliq Simone

polity

Copyright © AbdouMaliq Simone 2019

The right of AbdouMaliq Simone to be identified as Author of this Work has been asserted in accordance with the UK Copyright, Designs and Patents Act 1988.

First published in 2019 by Polity Press

Polity Press
65 Bridge Street
Cambridge CB2 1UR, UK

Polity Press
101 Station Landing
Suite 300
Medford, MA 02155, USA

All rights reserved. Except for the quotation of short passages for the purpose of criticism and review, no part of this publication may be reproduced, stored in a retrieval system or transmitted, in any form or by any means, electronic, mechanical, photocopying, recording or otherwise, without the prior permission of the publisher.

ISBN-13: 978-1-5095-2335-1
ISBN-13: 978-1-5095-2336-8 (pb)

A catalogue record for this book is available from the British Library.

Cover image: *Venu*, 2012, By: Asim Waqif, Indian, founded in 1978; Bamboo, cotton and jute rope, tar. interactive electronics; Length x width x height: 426.8 x 548.8 x 426.8 cm (14 x 18 x 14 ft.), work will be reconfigured on site; Collection Galerie Daniel Templon, Paris, Brussels; L-SE 1204.8.1

Typeset in 11 on 13pt Sabon LT Std by Servis Filmsetting Ltd, Stockport, Cheshire
Printed and bound in Great Britain by Clays Ltd, Elcograf S.p.A.

The publisher has used its best endeavours to ensure that the URLs for external websites referred to in this book are correct and active at the time of going to press. However, the publisher has no responsibility for the websites and can make no guarantee that a site will remain live or that the content is or will remain appropriate.

Every effort has been made to trace all copyright holders, but if any have been inadvertently overlooked the publisher will be pleased to include any necessary credits in any subsequent reprint or edition.

For further information on Polity, visit our website:
politybooks.com

Contents

Acknowledgements

Gratitude is extended to: the Smuts Fund of Cambridge University for sponsoring the three lectures on which this monograph is based; Gautam Bhan of the Indian Institute for Human Settlements, who provided invaluable advice and support for organizing the manuscript and providing logistical support for work in India; Anant Maringanti and the Hyderabad Urban Lab, for hosting the residency program where much of the manuscript was written, and to Sushmita Pati, Priya Sen, and Tripta Chandola for their support for work in Delhi; Edgar Pieterse, Lisa Damon, John Thompson, and Morten Nielsen for reading various iterations of the manuscript, as well as the "Group of 20" colleagues and friends assembled at Cambridge University on November 16, 2017, to review the project; Rika Febriyani, for her collaboration on every aspect of this project; and, above all, Ash Amin, for making this all possible and for his belief in me.

For
Zaira Cheyenne Simone and Na'ilah Xazaar Simone

I

The Uninhabitable

The uninhabitable: those "lands of no one" (McKittrick 2013: 6). Lands that embodied inferiority and, once appropriated and settled through colonization, were further specified as the exclusive purview of those whose emplacement was to be considered "incongruous with humanness" (McKittrick 2013: 7). Katherine McKittrick asks, in the context of the plantation, whether or not that which was defined as lifeless perhaps points to simply a different form of life embedded in a range of "secretive histories" (2013: 10).

> How we live is finally not that important; that we live is… (Moten 2017: 191)

> It hurts to live always undone and unfinished. It is heartbreaking. It is heartbreaking even when the impossibility is joyful or you catch a glimpse of a life outside that inflexible weight. (McKittrick and Weheliye 2017: 28)

Districting Somewhere

For several decades, my stepdaughter has occupied a two-room flat in a dreary mass of apartment blocks in

the Algiers suburb, Les Eucalyptus. She is fond of pointing out that she lives in a world on her own surrounded
by glassy-eyed neighbors with far-away looks. They
are not really there; they do not adhere to any script,
she says. Their eyes are on prizes somewhere else. Each
neighbor has different destinations in mind. Even when
they navigate the same routines of drudgery, going to
useless jobs, to markets short on everything, and to
municipal buildings rife with conspiracies, they never
take the same steps twice; they always alter the route.

Even on the single hallway in her building of chipped
concrete, the dealers, the Salafists, and those who are
devout about nothing in particular don't so much carve
out territory but allow paths to be constantly crossed so
that there is nothing recognizable to defend. If the police
and their bevy of hangers-on report infractions, then the
proliferation of possible mistakes that residents make
never repeating the same routine twice turn everyday life
into something nearly impossible to police. Yet simple
courtesies and signs of respect are offered no matter how
profound the fundamental disagreements about the basic
life orientations. The repetition of prayer, intoxication,
petty scams, and household chores induces a haze of tolerance, allowing the most minimal of actions to provoke
small but pliable alterations in the unfolding of a day or
night and the prospects or dangers this might bring.

All of the residents are convinced of big people behind
the scenes. They can even sometimes name names. But
they are also skeptical of their convictions. Ever attentive of each other, regardless of whoever they have
thrown their lot in with, the profusion of words, gossip,
stories, and impressions make up their bets on shaping
the near future, indifferent though they may be as to
what that future actually consists of.

For, in such districts, existing under permanent sus-
picion and suspension, it is important to manufacture

evidence that can be sifted through for clues that point to culprits in all directions; where the attentiveness of gazes, so vital to keep everyone in line, can't look everywhere at once, and so small gaps open for a quick deal, a quick fuck, a quick way out. This is not a world, my stepdaughter says, that is inhabitable.

Those who wear the pants may be weakly united in their need to occupy the public sphere, to mark out a domain amidst a landscape of dilapidated cafés, mechanic sheds, and tin-can-laden corner groceries. But Les Eucalyptus is a district of endless favors, sincere and feigned respect for those with the semblance of any kind of connection. Silently, the occasional young woman keeps her head down, resists the temptations of domestic dramas and household problem solving to finish enough school to get salaried somewhere. The financing for a new mosque or two may suddenly appear from disputed sources, but the pipes in most flats leak and often run dry. There are few repairs. Neighbors hear everything and know little about what to make of it.

Again, it is not that collective denial or stasis rules. For despite the stereotypes, the public and private are subject to oscillating inversions. Sitting in a café may be the only opportunity to be alone, even when, especially at night, all of the tables are taken. "Holding up the walls," as is the common expression for unemployed men, may indeed actually hold something up, as in intercept, block, or sustain. For the walls that divide domestic spaces, the purview largely of women, are not just porous sieves of information but marks of complex geographies where bonds and cuts in webs of lateral relations are made.

All of the doors that open and close a hundred times a day where nothing tangible seems to be exchanged, all of the stairs that are climbed up and down even when no doors are opened, all of the turning of the next corner, the hesitations between school, shop, mosque, and home, all of the shared taxis hailed to reach the next kilometer, all make up the rhythms whereby Les Eucalyptus is turned inside out and back.

The question of holding is important. No matter how improvised, lives need to be held, supported. They need a somewhere in which to take place, and places need to be assessed in terms of what they are able to hold. But to hold easily mutates into a form of capture, and if urban life comes to depend upon improvisation, the holding cannot take the form of a strictly notated score. It cannot keep a strict count; it can't make some lives count more or less than others. For when improvisation takes off, one direction cannot count as more generative than any other; this uncertainty is part of the risk of such composition. Additionally, a somewhere must hold the "secretive histories" that McKittrick refers to in the chapter's opening lines; it must hold a darkness that provides cover for experiments residents may initiate but are not yet ready to commit fully to. A somewhere must proportion exposure and opacity.

So, improvised lives require a somewhere, and in this book I will look at this somewhere as *districts*, as places capable of holding an intensive heterogeneity of lives and ways of doing things, but which also do not hold residents down to specific regimens of discipline or anticipation. Rather, they attempt to hold residents to each other just enough to enable an atmosphere of mutual witnessing, to hold residents to an ethic of letting others go their own way without that way being seen as having dire implications for anyone else. Residents are then held in an atmosphere of things continuously being worked out and proportioned. An atmosphere of countervailing, complementary, and incommensurable measures that gives rise to a specific, yet changing sense of place.

This is a book situated in districts. Or more, precisely, it is a book about *districting*. By districting, I mean a process of creating a platform for operating in the world using a repertoire of available classifications and administrative categories to set out a terrain that is then turned into something that exceeds all efforts to definitively pin it down, to contain what it can do. This surfeit of experience provides the opportunity for residents to write themselves into a milieu that otherwise might seem to marginalize them and their ways of doing things. It is a process that aims less to make a particular place inhabitable than it does to enable residents to spiral in and out, propel themselves into the larger urban surrounds and then bear back down again into the familiar places now rendered unfamiliar. It is the creation of a rhythm of itineraries that are themselves uninhabitable.

Let us take a well-known example of districting in the work of Sun Ra. For Sun Ra, going back in time, Egypt was the touchstone for what would become a complex interweaving of mythology, numerology, space travel, theosophy, Black nationalism, and the occult. Nominally a jazz musician who managed huge "arkestras" over a long career that folded in every type of music and sound imaginable, Sun Ra's commitment was to a "Black knowledge society" – a technical capacity for going into the future as an extra-planetary urbanization. While the metaphors of Saturn and outer space permeated the representations of such an urbanization, what was intended beyond such metaphors was the technical realization of the imaginations and capacities Blacks honed in their great migration to the cities of the North from the hardscrabble rural tenancies of the South and the repressive Jim Crow practices that sought to keep them at the peripheries of Southern towns and cities.

This movement between the mythic pasts of Blackness and its future realization beyond the earth seemingly unable to accommodate it was Sun Ra's persistent practice of districting. But he was also engaged in much more prosaic efforts in this regard. When Sun Ra showed up in Chicago after the Second World War, there had already been several decades where Blacks of different residential histories and class backgrounds had worked hard to use the sheer presence of Black bodies in the city – their looks, voices, movements, rhythms, appetites, sexualities, and strivings – to build economies that enabled some measure of autonomy from subservience and resistance to marginalization. Racialized apparatuses of control came down hard on these efforts, and Sun Ra encountered a Chicago that put a squeeze on trade unions, the political left, radical organizations, as well as outlets of popular culture – show venues, media, and radio.

It was at this point that the emphasis on Black knowledge as technical operations took hold in Sun Ra's project. Black people did not go through all they went through just in order to be integrated into the terms of an American society that did everything possible to keep them out. After having acquired a substantial history of being in cities, of proving that there could be something like a "Black city" itself, extra-ordinary, "extra-planetary" efforts were required in order to concretize these attainments.

From street pamphleteering, small book imprints, records, and performances that crossed swing, bop, blues, show tunes, and experimental improvisation, appearances at strip clubs, weddings, concert halls, street parties, jazz clubs, circuses, and universities, and the intersection of intensive musical and philosophical experimentation with novelty entertainment and nods to the full gamut of Black associational life, Sun Ra and his large bands and associates tried to become a *district* in themselves. This was not just improvised expression, but a process of intensive study (Sites 2012).

For Sun Ra, then, districting referred to an incessantly inventive practice of operating in the discontinuities between having a location in which one is identified and from which one can identify and speak to others *and* the capacity to address others, call upon them, and implicate them beyond the specificity of any location. As such, Egypt did not hold anything in itself, it was not a promise ready to spring into any kind of revolutionary action, but more a device that could relay the knowledge Sun Ra said that Blacks needed toward aspirations that continuously had to find different masks under which to operate, and also away from the strict codifications of what could be counted. For Sun Ra, it didn't matter that much if Black people were missing from inhabiting American urban life; what was more important was that they went "missing in action."

A Human Surge

Amidst the competing choruses of exaggeration and indifference, of longings for extinction and desperate boosts of immune systems, something surges forward and back. The surge is both power failure and inexplicable excess; it jumps scales while sometimes eliminating anything to fall back on. It is a strange rhythm neither reconcilable to ancient cyclic times nor acceleration. This is a rhythm perhaps best exemplified in Eduardo Williams' film, *The Human Surge* (2016). Wavering indiscernibly between documentary and fiction, youth in Buenos Aires, Maputo, and Isla Bohol (Philippines) are depicted as incessantly in motion, seemingly aimless even as many of them have steady jobs. They search for free Wi-Fi hotspots, Internet cafés, and ways to turn on-line activity into money.

In the first two cities, young men attempt to modulate the willful exposure of their bodies on Internet sites that offer particular amounts of money to see flesh. They are not good at this game, and they don't care. The recesses of the web do not hold their attention as much as do the prolific spaces of relative abandonment and infrequent visitation that dot their cities but that are not yet ruins. They talk about obscure theories of genomes and mathematics, witchcraft and far-off galaxies, the possibilities of pre-natal memories and future predilections, moving from one quick obscure observation to another. Impossible to stand still, always equipped with cellphones, but sometimes fixated on the slightest shift in light, in the movements of ants, the film's youth constantly engage a domain larger than the immediate surrounds even as they seemingly occupy a marginal position within it.

Here, the surge as rhythm emerges from attempts to reach beyond the confines of limited places and routines, and yet retains a microscopic view of the constantly surprising details about the places that could be left behind. This is a rhythm of endurance, of surging forward and withdrawing. It is not a rhythm of endless becoming nor of staying put; it is making the most of the "hinge," of knowing how to move and think through various angles while being fully aware of the constraints, the durability of those things that are "bad for us" (Stoler 2016).

For, as Williams' film clearly demonstrates, individuals always have to work out a sense of proportionality, even when things cannot be made proportionate in any clear, definitive way. What is it about themselves and their capacities which are to be extended to particular others and what do these acts of self-extending indicate about what is being withheld, in part, as a lure to incite the engagement of others? This working out of proportionality is not merely the calculations of self-interest. It is also the sculpting of a field of affordances that shape the connections, interdependencies, and autonomies persons conceive and operationalize with each other. So, any notion of the *social* is always "out of joint," never assumed as a stabilized whole. Rather, it is an ongoing deformation of systemic entities, as individuals are the carriers of social affordances and memory, and societies are the parts of ongoing transformations of personhood (Corsín Jiménez 2008) – a scale without scale.

Such scale without scale can be seen across many Southern districts of the urban poor, where the South becomes something to be crossed, a "cross to bear," a something "over there" that bears weighty appellations: "We are the ones that God forgot," "We have become dogs," or "This is the middle of nowhere." These are targeted populations (Parks 2016), ones that must be kept in line by being forgotten or kept in the crosshairs, or in analyses where hairsplitting questions about "what are these populations really?" prevail. The appellations deem these spaces uninhabitable, not fit for human habitation, environments full of toxicity and violence, fast and slow.

But in these designations, there is a certain detachment, a detachment from the imperative to compare, to be viewed within the hierarchies of sufficiency or sustainability. If God has truly forgotten these places, then perhaps there is a kind of freedom not to be remembered by or incorporated into God's analytics. For in environs full of everyday catastrophe, the only way to live with it is to attain some indifference, where all that which is capable of producing an unjustifiable or unnecessary death – when each death is necessary and therefore justified – is flattened out. Where it becomes an even surface that carries the marks of every event, but at the same time does not distinguish among them.

The very conditions that would seem to condemn residents to obvious hardship take on, in such a detachment, a more minimal operation (Laruelle 1999) in that they no longer solely point to that hardship but simply are what they are, and thus able to become elements of a broader sense of interactions. They become marks without meaning, lines of scarification on bodies prepared for battle, prayer, sex, and repose – not only the death to which they seem normatively consigned.

We may see many of the world's urban districts as uninhabitable. But is what makes them uninhabitable only the obvious conditions of violence, oppression, and toxicity that are their predominant characterizations? What if something else were at work? What if, besides being a descriptor of the ways in which these districts are scenes of a crime, a crime against the humanity of their residents, the uninhabitable was also a method, not one necessarily chosen by residents, but rather something converted into a method from the shards of broken lives and broken infrastructures that make up a district's heritage. What if the uninhabitable enabled a kind of thinking that challenged or refused what it means to viably inhabit a place? What if it was a method to more fully understand the *rhythms of endurance*, the surges of life that carry bodies forward and back between destinations that are altered in each approach, each retreat? So here I want to explore the uninhabitable as a method to think about these *rhythms of endurance*.

A Lure for (Yet) Another South

In terms of its role as method, I want to look at the uninhabitable as a lure, how it draws one into a place and situation in a way that does not describe or account for it. Rather, it pulls one into its shifting terrain, fuzzy boundaries, its vibrations and rhythms that cannot be contained by any spatial structure. No component, no entity of the place stands out more than any other. Mud walls, broken concrete, oil spills, toxic fumes, riven bodies, stomped feet, wild gestures, attentive gazes – all of these elements dance with each other as curling smoke, momentary anthems, sometimes embracing each other as repeated refrains in the cold mornings and anxious nights. Everything is packed into a density of contact, of the discrepant rubbing up against each other in multiple frictions, sparks that ignite chain reactions, the webs of many crammed causations looking out for any possible vehicle of release. The heterogeneous shapes and economies of poor and working-class districts, segmented and distinctly inscribed across urban fabrics though they may be, make up specific machines. These machines produce contexts along the way, along the way of things passing through each other, of bodies passing by, of failed lives passing out of view, of scenarios and conclusions passing into something else.

The explorations of this book largely concern what was formerly known as the Global South, a world within a world that has disappeared as a world, if it ever indeed was a world. Perhaps the South was a world by default. It was the forcible enclosure wrought by a head without a body, then looking for a body anywhere, as the impetus for colonization, a practice that destroyed worlds by assuming natives did not have any (Neyrat 2016). So, to deem something uninhabitable was to make it available to interventions of all kinds, and particularly interventions that would operate at a distance, that sought to affect things by being removed from them; to operate as a body in the abstract; to manipulate but not feel (Satia 2014).

So the South I want to invoke here is a South not so much as a conceptual designation, not so much a residue of political aspiration or legacy, but something closer to science fiction, something made up as it goes along, not dissimilar to the chronopolitics of the Afrofuturists. This long-standing series of projects by Black people to write themselves into a future foreclosed to them cycles back in time in order to recuperate materials, unreal yet enduring fictions, to imagine non-human futures devoid of racial tropes.

All passages, to avoid becoming voids of the middle, still have to take place along corridors. They still need vehicles of transit, for even djinns and ghosts have geographies. And so the South becomes latitude defined not so much by common colonial demise or recuperation, not so much by a look or a specific modality of sensuousness, but a form of passage, of residents trying to reach each other even if they may have only vague ideas about each other. In the *Human Surge*, youthful men in Buenos Aires and Maputo become dimly aware of each other. Through the ongoing commodification of their black and brown bodies, they become aware of being in the same boat.

Of course, there are many "Global Souths" (Robinson 2016). Some are extensions of old and new imperial powers, some are emerging imperial or, at least, dominant regional powers as well. Some Southern cities far exceed in technical capacity anything concretized in the "North." Construction booms rest uneasily with deepening impoverishment; spectacular built environments are coupled with intense predation; socioeconomic inequalities can be staggering. Cities are torn between becoming mirrors of everywhere and amplifying a distinctiveness that sometimes proves to be simply the repetition of an injunction to be different. Oscillating conjunctions based on religion, race, language, and regional identity provide signature architectures of circulation and enclosure. Financial investments penetrate nearly everywhere, with high-risk investments in "dangerous" atmospheres promising the inordinate riches that have long characterized supposedly remote or empty regions. Populations at risk are increasingly seen as such because they fail to take on sufficient volumes of the right kind of risk. Development curves can simultaneously fall below and exceed all expectations.

Urbanization is replete with spatial operators, where space is an informational system equipped with routines, formats, and formulas that generate repeatable products such as housing developments, industrial zones, consumption, and leisure centers. Combined with proliferating digital technologies, urban spatial production becomes subject to forms of calculation that circumvent political negotiation, infuse places with a surfeit of trends and possibilities that require narrow bands of expertise to sort out (Easterling, 2016)

At the same time, hyperlocal networks and apps are collaboratively designed to enable peer communities to advance local interests by sharing human and physical resources. Urbanization is something increasingly characterized by open source autonomous logistics infrastructure, technologies to mitigate anthropogenic effects on climate, an expanding urban sensorium of interlinked sensors registering data at more fine-grained temporalities, and interoperable data. It seems increasingly difficult to discern a specifically human surge.

Yet, despite these developments, there is a "South" that concerns how residents pass in and out of all of the histories that attempt to generalize them, such as the appellations that saw Mumbai, Jakarta, Salvador, and Lagos as "Black cities," or that saw specific urbanities as "informal" or predominated by slum conditions. So here, the South is the concretization of the simultaneous emergence and impossibility of worlding, of a concrete darkness that provides a home for impossible socialities that nevertheless assume an inscription, materialize lines of flight, attack, and articulation "grooving" the terrain.

The Evening of Spiraling Darkness

In the scores of working-class districts within which I have worked and lived over the past decades, there may be a straightforward and incremental line of progress in living conditions that has been attained when measured as an aggregate of life trajectories. But when broken down as stories of individual and household lives over the course of time, this aggregate of progress has been realized through wild fluctuations in these very individual stories, of often inexplicable ups and downs, stories of sudden accumulation and loss, luck and catastrophe that have dispossessed individuals of stable orientations and operational platforms, that have pushed people far and wide, as well as pushed others into narrow crevices. That which would seem to tear a district apart is sometimes at work as its guarantor of a plausible statistical mean. And sometimes districts are simply torn apart, especially when simple "meanness" dominates, where the "mean" is one barrio boss with an empty taco shell left standing.

All then seem to be evened out in an analytical gaze that pitches itself to some average story, that gathers up all of the statistical indices possible to assign to these oscillations, which considers communities marching in step along one route, one line. Progress becomes the normalization of sharing protocols and algorithmic design that figures its way across large data sets in order to support locational decisions, balance urban processes, and maximize economic multiplier effects and sustainability.

The economic entity – the district, community, or region – that progresses is constituted through these measurements as a collective subject. But it is a subject not made up of stable components, but rather components that are passing through each other at different speeds and capacities – some on the way "up," some on the way "down," and some entrained in more circuitous routings. So that the individual identity pointed to in the story of that collective subject is itself "re-routed" into a more linear narrative, a kind of shape-shifting made up of fluctuating disjunctions between the deployment of "I" as some kind of stable referent and its shifting uses as pointing to a varied manifestation in different contexts (Gerlitz and Lury 2014; MacKenzie 2015). The collective attainment is not one of a collection of clearly defined individuals "but a moving (exchange) ratio, of more-and-less-than ones, in which authenticity, belief, doubt and speculation are the always contingent outcome of a serial calibration of signal and noise, interference and (un)certainty" (Lury 2018).

In these districts of the poor and working class across the South where I have worked, significant dimensions of the "lives" of the elements that make up these districts then appear to address no specific concerns or targets. They conjoin rhythms of occasions and practices not easily attributed to any single person or thing. They are rather shifters in a complex politics that may use the occasion of specific enunciations actualized in particular circumstances to create contexts for bringing provisional collectives to life, ones that don't pin down their constituents to overbearing judgments or histories. These contexts enable endurance, not for the durability of clearly knowable entities that must be defended or liberated at all costs, but for endurance to be something that is felt, where what was aspired to, what was sacrificed for, what was the compelling imagination of all the strivings and hard work of care is not lost.

In circumstances of intense volatility and uncertainty – circumstances that characterize many urban districts across the South – it is important for residents not to draw too much attention to themselves, to not stand out, particularly if they enjoy advantages that others may not have, if they prompt envy or exude a constant sense of dependency. At the same time, residents cannot be viewed as simply adding to the repetition of an endless grind of drudgery and dissolution. They cannot situate themselves as merely expendable, a surplus of suffering. They must become a small niche of exception, of adding something different to the fabric of mere survival but in such a way as to be able to control the demands made of this singularity, always vulnerable to depletion. How to calibrate these measures of dissimilitude and daring, these efforts to blend in and to exceed that norm, where each maneuver risks a debilitating cost, could easily flip to its other side? How to not get double bound by the exigency to play things "both ways"?

These require astute observations that involve multiple angles, require particular ways of moving through grimy lanes, overbearing domestic disputes, random violence, and the ideology of the street. The lives of residents must ramify, but in ways not easily traced back to them but which nevertheless open corridors for these same residents to keep moving. Here, experiments to make something happen spiral out and in, bear down and ramify outwards, not in clear direct channels of affecting, but in wavy, circuitous lines. This does not simply offer an approximate description of the way resident maneuvers ramify, but also point to the incessant search for positions from which to observe the swarm of these maneuvers across the landscape of apparent drudgery and danger. It is seeking positions where a person becomes more than one and less than two.

Here, what would seem to render everything about a particular district just one more piece of toxicity becomes a strategic device to occlude the lengths that residents go to in order to observe something differently, something tentative and momentary. Thus domestic workers in rich households, janitors in multinational headquarters, security guards in research installations, drivers of the elite, toilet cleaners in airports, enforcers for local politicians, rogue police, mechanics affixing false compartments on delivery trucks, pirate electricity connectors, cardsharps, Pentecostal pastors, button stitchers, sewer technicians, shamans, fabricators, counterfeiters, and hackers all spiral around each other and their respective places of operation.

In their dancing around and with each other, they destabilize and articulate, enfold and detach. They are simultaneously the substrate of all urban productivity and the detritus. While it is unjust that so many must stake their sustenance on complex collaborations, actions vulnerable to breakage, excess demands and hopes, and that involve too many variables, it is also unjust to reduce the work that does get done to simple generalizations about predation.

Whenever this substrate of residents can convert their abstract sense of not being alone, of not being suspended in the precarity of their jobs behind the wheel, besides the switch, cleaning the corridors of power, into a felt sense of solidarity, they might trip up the entire "show." Nothing in their behaviors is aligned, matched up for sure. Nothing rules anything out definitively in rhythms of incessant turbulence. They might not bring down the city, but they are in most respects able to bring down the city to the requirements of their makeshift economies that effect a modest but real redistribution of goods and services to their residencies otherwise formally cut off or excessively disciplined.

These are not matters of "spontaneous flow" but of calibration and measure. It is about residents passing by, measuring themselves up along whatever is momentarily gathered, employing all kinds of makeshift measures to regulate proximity and distance. Measures consist of many devices, ways of seeing, and calculating, many operating according to a "strange" mathematics. Rhythm is produced from these measures, from the efforts of the connected and disconnected to create refrains, momentary stabilities that offer up a repertoire of vernaculars, gestures, and sensibilities that can then be taken up to twist and turn a place into some malleable yet steady arena for people to pay attention to each other, engage each other, or not.

A built environment is shaped from and for various itineraries of movement. It is anticipated and parsed into varying measures and used by different constellations and densities of actors and things. It is a built environment that generates a rhythm of both convergence and detachment. This convergence and detachment is increasingly aided and abetted by home-grown "cosmotechnics" (Hui 2016b) – autoconstructed telephony networks, YouTube-disseminated realities, self-built condo timeshares, conditional cash transfers, moneyless credit systems, and rough-hewn blockchain-ledgered accountability. The slums are full of machines.

Detachment offers some protection against a porosity that brings too many things to bear on any place or occasion. The irony of toxicity is that it sometimes affords the stability of predictable, ongoing social interchange, and production of a supportive interior for the continuity of a set of social ties. Polluted streams and industrial stink can sometimes create virtuous boundaries. For, too many crossroads end up pushing things aside. At the same time, too many firm enclosures atrophy the competencies of residents. Suture and detachment have to be taken, but there are no clear equal measures, opening and closing is always a risk (Roberts 2017).

Composition and Refusal

The rhythms of endurance are not about the resilience of human life, about the never-ending resourcefulness of a subaltern imagination. It is not about a virtuous general ecology that, in the end, works out a functional recalibration of elements each diminished in their own terms, each insufficient to the replenishment of the other. Rather, in a rupture of organicity (Wills 2016), endurance also entails the actions of bodies indifferent to their own coherence, where bodies proliferate a churning that staves off death in their extension toward a liveliness of things in general, and where bodies become a transversal technology, as gesture, sex, gathering, and circulation operate as techniques of prolonging.

How many actions are undertaken seemingly indifferent to the survival of the subject that undertakes them, which instead takes these subjects under? When bodies speak, spit, stomp, fuck, gesture, lunge, or hover, they become technical forces, and, as such, bodies are conveyors of artifice that may represent nothing in particular. Intersections of this artifice, gestures crossing gestures, are not measures of what bodies do, not practices of bordered bodies acting within specific environments. Rather, they amplify the dispersal of intensities across various places, where everyday experience is not something holed up in some makeshift protective encasing called the house, however it might be constructed, but all of the ways residency was instantiated under radars, in provisional layouts, in mass-produced real estate schemes or improvised shelters. The form of residing is always a desperate punctuation of a crossing of undomesticated forces that cannot be measured by income levels, personality tests, medical exams, or means testing.

Here the uninhabitable is that constant refrain that seeks to create contexts of operation that cannot be stabilized as points of anchorage, as settlements to inhabit, even though the refrain, itself, is a stabilizing repetition. It is rather a decoupling of home from habitation, the making of a home that cannot extend itself into any discernible horizon and that, instead, must be discarded or carried on backs or become the guiding source of imagination. For the intersections among spiraling trajectories are a matter of care (Puig de la Bellacasa 2011), inexplicable care, rogue care, care on the run, a tending not to people or by people, but a care that precedes them. It is a care that makes it possible for residents to navigate the need to submit and exceed, submerge themselves into a darkness in which they are submerged but to read its textures, its tissues, to see something that cannot be seen. It enables them to experience the operations of a sociality besides, right next to the glaring strictures of their obligations, expulsions, and exploitation, something that enables endurance, not necessarily their own endurance as human subjects, but the endurance of care indifferent to whatever or whoever it embraces.

This is a process that entails both composition and refusal. To use the example of the Art Ensemble of Chicago, it is a matter of composing the conditions that facilitate improvisation and dialogue among the players. It is also the creation of a platform that not only enfolds bits and pieces of the legacies of Black music and their interfaces with multiple soundscapes, notations, and institutions, but compresses, distorts, and stretches them to release an untold energy that propels a different kind of "message for our folks," a different trajectory of historical time. Here, the "people of sorrow" are addressed with the gathering up of laments, invocations, assertions, pleas, prayers, lullabies, trances, and exultations that assumed various modalities, which were the emanations of particular circumstances and then reworked, rewoven with a vast range of instrumentation into a home without home.

The cut, the earthquake in Black music at the beginning of the 1960s, that period which corresponded to a significant postcolonial moment in Africa, was signaled by Coltrane's *Giant Steps* and Ornette Coleman's *The Shape of Jazz to Come*. Here was another kind of surge, as Kodowo Eshun (1998) describes the evolution of this cut four years later in 1965, "Ascension's surges, like those on Ornette Coleman's Free Jazz or Egyptian Empire's The Horn, build towards planes when all the horns synch in a power surge, the belching exhaust fumes of a colossal rocket as it tilts into the air like a vertical city."

Within the new compositional and improvisational structures, it was possible to figure out how the ensemble "left home," left the recognizable melody, but nearly impossible to tell how the return home was navigated, back to the familiar chord changes. Joseph Jarman, reed player with the Art Ensemble of Chicago and founding member of the Association for the Advancement of Creative Musicians, would describes this as a process of "getting carried away." No longer would Black people be interested in pretending that there was a home for Blackness in this world. As Black folk were carried away to America, they would then carry themselves away without destination; they would carry themselves.

Katherine McKittrick (2016) says this act of carrying is a matter of generating rhythms and waveforms that emanate from the densities of heterogeneous activities and forces, elaborating multiple registers of sound impacting upon neurophysiological circuits that modulate affect, sympathy, and a preparedness to act. Such sonic atmospheres are infrastructures for the enunciation of the exaltation required for collaborative practices – the sense of wonderment and ease required to live-with the ebbs and flows, the constraints and traumas of everyday life.

There is also an element of refusal here, a refusal for exclusionary inclusion, and inclusionary exclusion (Campt 2012). It's the refusal to be a subject to a law that refuses to recognize you. Rights act to absorb the margins into the realm of what is perceived to be normal. The politics of dis-identification is instead about refusing to be represented in a "right" and be accounted for that. It is about non-reductionism. This is what Stephenson and Papadopoulos (2006) call "outside politics." It is a politics defined not by opposition or necessarily resistance, but instead a refusal of the very premises that have historically negated, for example, the lived experience of Blackness as either pathological or exceptional to the logic of white supremacy.

It is a refusal of a relation that denies composition. Whereas composition entails gradations – more or less timbre, charting, stricture, and improvisation – these gradations are not fixed. The ensemble contributes to the evolution of the sound in ways that don't weigh their relative value. So Jarman's is not a refusal to be composed, because composition retains the relative autonomy of its components. They remain aspects of other compositions. All the characteristics and potentials of the components that go into a composition need not be what they are when they are incorporated into it. What is refused is the fixing, the chaining of elements to a particular compositional structure, the refusal of the imperative to relate.

What is refused is to become solely or primarily a "problem to be solved" or a "people to be liberated or developed." As Marcos Camacho (2017), aka Marcola of Brazil's extra-parliamentary Primer Comando de la Capital, states: "No more proletariat, or unhappy people, or oppressed. There is a third thing growing out there, raised in the mud, educated through sheer illiteracy, getting their own diplomas on the street, like a monstrous Alien hidden under the crevasses of the city. A new language has already sprung. We are at the center of the unsolvable."

The uninhabitable, then, also exists detached from being a problem that needs to be solved, something that permits all of the multitude of small efforts deployed by residents of poor and working-class districts to be something *besides* compensations, impulsive gestures, violent outbursts, or claustrophobic routines. It is also a refusal to participate in institutions which function largely to attribute failure to the behavior of their constituents.

Of course, refusal has its limits given the way that speculative destruction has long constituted the underpinnings of capital accumulation through urbanization (Brenner 2013; Harvey 1989). The production of space itself has become key to capitalist accumulation (Aalbers 2011; Harvey 2012), and urban rent, as the abstraction of the collectively produced heterogeneity of sociality and used as a privately held asset, is one of the most valued commodities (Hardt and Negri 2008). Curated unaffordability, disinvestment, overt erasure, expulsion, segregation, and social disentanglement have long been the familiar tools for making space uninhabitable. They are the all too familiar vocabularies of damming and unleashing urban churn. Huge volumes of cement, bricks, mortar, and steel are deployed to structure the intersections of countervailing forces that always have been what the city is, and then demolished as insufficient containers of value seeking other venues and calculations. In the interstices of the continual remaking of the built environment as asset, hundreds of millions of residents are suspended in provisional formats of work and residence.

Urban majorities may have always been complicit with such speculative destruction. Yet, in part, this complicity was a by-product of the ways in which the prevailing logics of self-construction, which emphasized continuous adaptations to the inherent volatility of urban life and to the unanticipated implications of the very efforts and initiatives of the majority, were forced into sedentary, defensive maneuvers. They increasingly had to operate through skewed patronage systems and murky political games in order to protect themselves. They were forced to hold too many different activities for too many persons; they often were left to fend for themselves in increasingly hostile policy frameworks and disattentive municipal institutions. They were rendered anachronisms, leftovers, replete with discordant and confusing ways of generating livelihood and habitation. The working and lower middle classes that largely drove the real economy of cities were repeatedly subject to punitive extractions, surveillance, and systematic neglect.

Districts that seemingly exude viable densities of residential, commercial, and public use are then jettisoned for imaginations of a more middle-class lifestyle in faceless vertical developments. Pursuit of increased consumption, belief in security through asset attainment, and a systematic tending to more individualized concerns and aspirations certainly exert substantial spatial reorderings, especially as these aspirations are saddled with debt.

Certainly, there is substantial evidence garnered across urban situations of the incessant and accelerated disentanglement of complex residential ecologies. While the exigencies of sustainability have indeed produced a wide range of fortuitous calculations – of the design and emplacement of built environments, of viable carbon footprints, material flows and energy use – the inability to make inhabitation work is not a matter of insufficient knowledge but rather political design. It is a continuous parasitic depletion of the capacities of the majority in favor of the conceits of an elite and its shadow world intent upon the circumscription of democratic life and the "desocialization of the common" (Hardt and Negri 2008).

Yet, here too, the majority may refuse any clear organization of sense, refuses any clear disposition of virtuous interests and futures. In many instances it refuses consolidation, and there is no denying the debilitating scenarios that this refusal unleashes. Such prospects remain a vital incentive for political mobilizations aimed at shaping the judicious operations of institutions and infrastructures. Still, a certain detachment from convictions that the virtuous is restored through recognizing our proper place within complex ecologies or jurisdictions may be necessary in order to fully appreciate the ways in which cities are full of many different kinds of forces. These forces do not necessarily rule out the ability of people to stay in place but require such stability to be a function of circular dispersals and returns, of constant exiting and re-entering through side doors.

As Claire Colebrook (2014) argues, inscription (and thus inhabitation) in its most basic maneuver remains the marking of something through its corresponding nothingness, of the civilized against the uncivilized, and so forth. Inscription is the tool of cutting. Once something is defined against what it is not, that "what it is not" is then "cut loose" from that which has been differentiated, no matter how tied it may be to a conceptual, economic, or political dependency. It assumes the position of utter contingency, the being of anything whatsoever, despite the proliferations of narratives and spatial controls through which that which is differentiated is subjected. At the same time, how, she asks, would we read ourselves if we did not assume some kind of overarching spirit or meaning within whatever is inscribed, but rather like inert lines, like the weathering of a building or the weathering of a storm, as an endurance that persists without sense.

Fugitive Graces

Habitation is supported through shifting ecologies of relation, through analogical substitutions where the elements of conditions of sufficiency can assume different valences, substitutions, and compensations (Barber 2016). The elements making up these relations are elements that express a fundamental "likeness" for each other and underpin their "willingness" to recalibrate their functioning in terms of each other. This is the ecological relationship where differences turn to each other, translate themselves in terms of the other, and over which hangs the specter of an inclusive "we." The weak and the strong, the natural and unnatural – different though they may be – can participate in such a larger frame of commonality. The militancy of the subjugated can always be smoothed over through reference to a common humanity or the operation of translation that frames that militancy as an act of subjectivity, a subjectivity whose features might not be shared but where the capacity to be subject is.

So, what would happen if such analogies were cut? What would a radical detachment look like? A detachment that nevertheless is able to hold many things, but where there is no possibility to discern the differences among those things. Or, a kind of detachment that runs as a parallel track to relational ecologies, a track that is something else besides (right next to) the incessant imperative to understand how things relate. For detachment also indicates that by the time a certain life at the margins comes to be represented, it has already moved on somewhere else.

At the heart of urban life was the belief in the capacity of the human to operate according to the maximization of its position, and this required a notion of free will, of the ability to act freely amongst otherwise constraining interdependencies (Colebrook 2017). This freedom necessitated relegating certain bodies to the status of property, capable of circulating only through the transactional circuits of economic exchange and valuation. Can, then, any detachment of urban life from this dependency on subjugation be conducted in the language of freedom or autonomy? How might an insistence on freedom and autonomy occlude the ways in which working-class districts manage to maintain conditions that keep precarity at bay? How might it keep us from paying attention to a life of small attainments, modes of sociality embedded in a kind of darkness, difficult to empirically verify?

So, the uninhabitable is the lure that initially draws us into particular kinds of observations aimed at diminishing, devaluing, improving, and redeeming specific conditions of the urban. Yet, under the veneer of these observations and the kinds of realities they constitute runs another surface *besides* them. Here, the conditions viewed as uninhabitable produce a series of maneuvers, thousands of small experiments that attempt to provisionally reconcile the demands that residents submerge themselves into the sensibilities connoted by their destitution or expendability and, at the same time, emerge from those conditions to offer resources and sensibilities that are nothing on their own but are components of an oscillating tissue, a constantly changing ground of improvised "districts." In these districts, intersections amongst these small projects might take place as the panoply of "strange alliances."

What is created does not so much ground or orient, but constitutes a politics of making home on the run, a form of fugitive graces, where particular operational entities, enfolding the human into something besides itself, come to the fore through practices of care. This is not a world of analogies, not a world where what residents do with each other is easily translatable into some overarching term. It is a care that detaches as much as it connects, for it cares about the way in which residents of poor and working-class districts are forced into particular kinds of structural relationships, made into the labor or saviors in reserve, made to enunciate not only their own impossible habitation but that of the scene of the crime, whether the Capitaloscene or Anthropocene.

Ensemble Work

These different sensibilities of the uninhabitable operate as an ensemble, as an enactment of vision in immediate praxis, as experiment that may not go anywhere, which may easily implode and exist without guarantee. But they are a necessary means of addressing a world of constraint and closure in terms that cut across the coherence of that world. Out of place, they are still capable of "neighborly relations" and "strange alliances." It is an ensemble of music, suggested by actual ensembles, such as the Art Ensemble of Chicago or those of Ornette Coleman.

Chapter 2 of the book thus consists of a series of vignettes that suggest how ensembles constitute a tissue of conceptualization, a quilting of notions, and how this quilting is a rhythm, a text read rhythmically across and in the midst of a crisscross of patterns and fragments that retain their capacity to be components of various elsewheres. The vignettes of Jakarta, Freetown, Chicago, Naples, and Haiti suggest a movement through detachment, detachment as a way to move, never fully cohering a world or a life, but drawing attention to how connections can spiral in and out, taking any thing outside of its normative orbit. How to be detached from a world where everywhere is the scene of a crime, where the crime spirals out in ways that draw people back into the places they seek to leave behind? They suggest the ways in which endurance is a practice that does not remain in place; is not a matter of enduring a place. Rather, it seeks to address the way in which places unknown, somewhere out in the distance, have come to pass through wherever people find themselves. As such, there is an invitation, a gravitational pull that the person has also rhythmically induced. The vignettes draw attention to the ways in which endurance does not seek to arrive at confirmation of its attainment, but always seeks to postpone such a reckoning.

Ensembles do not play by themselves; they are situated somewhere; they rely upon the physicality of instruments and instrumentation for the players to address each other. The moving and stationary ensembles that gather and coalesce at the intersections of the needs to demonstrate both unequivocal solidarity and niche practices in poor and working-class districts require things as a means to design contexts – an underpass, a transit station, a causeway, a store. What are the materials of relations, the materiality of darkness, of vertical towers, of scrap metal, of crowded lanes, of apartment units occupied according to varying temporalities?

Chapter 3 then explores how endurance concerns the mechanics of relations; a mechanics of being in relations when it is not unequivocally certain just what is being related. It is a matter of partial connections, of finding ways to extract and extrude elements of things as components of experimental bodies or entities, as contexts in which to operate, and which do not need to profess loyalty to the integrity of normative categories – race, gender, religion, or class. Relations in rhythm, of how people and things come and go, involve themselves and withdraw. It is about the circumstances where people address what might be possible to do with what they have access to now; that not so much defend particular territories of interest but use the dispossessions they may experience in the intensified uncertainties of urban life in order to discover what might have been present and possible all along. But such discoveries require practices of care; where care becomes the most important gesture to endure situations when widely discrepant empirical realities are all equally possible.

Relations are concretized, not as the interaction of definitive substances or forms of life. Rather, they are concretized via the specific media or milieu in which they take place, the destination of the transmitted information, the name in which any messaging is enunciated, the content of that which is transmitted and its particular procedural codification (Hui 2016a). Each relationship can now be assigned a digital "address" and thus is available to reconfigurations that are also addressable, concretely situated within a web of recursive reticulation and named with predicates. Here, human operators assume no overarching plane or perspective, for they are fully within the system.

Entities such as citizens, denizens, ethnics, and institutions – while defined by their transactions with each other and entering into specific transactions based

on the various legal and cultural statuses of their personhood – retain "insides" that are continuously reshaped
through the application of various techniques, styliza-
tion, and the efforts to reconcile the frictions generated
by different operating systems which they are exposed
to and incorporated in (Riles 2010). Apropos the concerns of the book, the interiors of districts then can
manifest certain traits, functions, and responsibilities
given their relations with other entities in the city. But
they also retain large measures of contestation and rear-
rangement as far as what takes place inside them – in
terms of how to accomplish or persuasively pretend to
accomplish the functions, including mutual anticipation
and indebtedness, made known through these relations.

To endure conditions that require the rhythmic oscillations of contradictory orientations and needs, to
navigate relationships with those whose "surfaces" are
always partial, always partly withdrawn, always pro-
ceeding in different directions simultaneously, amplifies
the need for inscription. Or, they need at least the belief
that inscription and legibility are possible. Residents of
the districts that constitute the places of reflection in
this book need to be equipped with maps, maps that do
not so much represent a particular terrain but embody
both the decision to "set out," to embark with a deter-
mination informed by a clear seeing of pathways and
connections. Residents may operate in the dark about
knowing for sure what makes them feel the way they do,
of determining definitively what causes their situation
to be what it is. But even within this darkness, there is
more than impulsive wandering.

Chapter 4 then focuses on the provisional map-
making of the contours of environment, about how
residents mobilize things from the canvas of their imagination in practices of bricolage in order to constitute
ways of dealing with districts that are both all over the

place and stuck in place. This is a non-Euclidian politics of small yet continuous attainments, of maps that are incrementally constructed, that are inconclusive yet viable. The maps in any summary visualization may suggest a territory that is uninhabitable, that lacks all of the key signs of orientation, but yet they are maps. They are maps that seem to emerge from the darkness of uncertainty, but yet guide their users to the location of home.

Chapter 5 acts as a provisional conclusion. It attempts to point to a peripheral politics, a politics of the periphery to which urban majorities are increasingly consigned. Peripheries are sites of aspiration and dejection, where residency has been both voluntarily and involuntarily taken up. They are the results of eviction, ideological persuasion, wild imaginations, and pragmatic calculation. In the rush to convert urban cores into liquid assets and mono-functional derivatives, all kinds of built environments and populations have been crammed into the peripheries, propelling desperate attempts at insulation and exasperated concessions to embrace the messiness. Whatever romance the city offered has long been eroded, and the peripheries come to be less places in which to reside and more staging areas for diffuse operations whose itineraries, trajectories, compositions, and motivations are increasingly difficult to discern.

Thus, a complex politics of crossing, of getting in and out of the way, of moving from one part of an urban region to another begins to take shape and constantly shifts shape. It is not clear what this politics does exactly; it may seem deficient in so many ways in securing the normative attainments of rights and services. But given the possibility that the remaking of urban cores is simply a dress rehearsal for a much more insidious project on the part of a multifarious global elite to simply jettison themselves out of most earthly requirements for their survival, thus rendering the majority expendable, then such a peripheral politics is vital for the ways in which it doesn't show its cards, becomes nearly impossible to pin down. This isn't just leaving things unfinished, it is not giving in to the constant of being incomplete or under duress, but rather creating conditions in which the disparate might stick together – an ensemble.

2
Ensemble Work

The air of the thing that escapes enframing is what I'm interested in – an often unattended movement that accompanies largely unthought positions and appositions. What if the thing whose meaning or value has never been found finds things, founds things? What if the thing will have founded something against the very possibility of foundation and against all anti- or post-foundational impossibilities? What if the thing sustains itself in the absence or eclipse of meaning that withholds from the thing the horrific honorific of "object"? At the same time, what if the value of that absence or excess is given to us only in and by way of a kind of failure or inadequacy – or, perhaps more precisely, by way of a history of exclusion, serial expulsion, presence's ongoing taking of leave – the non-attainment of meaning or ontology, of source or origin. (Moten 2008: 182)

The notion of ensemble work, its strange "thing-ness," takes its cue from the concept of *harmolodics* that Ornette Coleman applied to his music. This is a way of playing where melody is not superseded by harmony, where the democracy of the ensemble was such that each player could deliver the melody in its own configuration of rhythm and chord changes. Harmolodic modulation is the method of moving the same notes-as-written from one clef to another in order to yield various names accompanied by a parallel modulation where the same notes are played on different instruments in order to realize various sounds.

So, the following vignettes operate as an ensemble. The ensemble will play out some of the variety of rhythms of endurance. The vignettes take up some of the notions applied in the discussion of the uninhabitable as method, notions such as "strange alliances," "spirals," "scenes of the crime," and "detachment." For now, the "players" in these vignettes will stay close to home, close to the places they come from, even if these places have been left behind a long time ago, to their own devices, without the players.

Strange Alliances

Ambassador and Kuningan ITC are attached 30-year-old malls set in the midst of the accelerated expansion of the central business district in Jakarta. Mega-towers now spread across decomposed working-class districts. The mall is full of small stores and is known for its supply of cheap electronics and software. It is always crowded with consumers actually shopping rather than simply soaking up the ambiance of a newer generation of malls. With the exception of the Carrefour supermarket, none of the outlets are parts of brand stores. The operation is largely managed by a collection of brokers orchestrating oscillating supply chains, managing intricate subcontracting arrangements over commercial space and use, and sculpting layers of complementarity among sellers, providers, and customers in ways that generate interacting specializations and piece together different scales of deals.

The Ambassador continues to thrive in ways that enfold many different sources of goods, types of knowledge, and networks of contact that keep prices affordable and customers engaged. But those who have worked the mall for a long time also point to a much more opaque and intricate space of operation that is situated in the dense strip of a popular neighborhood in Karbela that endures just outside the northern circumference of the mall's parking area. This densely packed old neighborhood, one of the few left in the area, is a repository of a different sort. Several of the brokers who actually manage the comings and goings of the Ambassador have their small houses here and help oversee an "archive" of stories presented by passers-by in search of family and friends gone missing, or conversely, in search of interventions for their inability to distance themselves from kin, lovers, and affiliations that always manage to know exactly where they can be found at any given time.

Passers-by also crowd small street-side eating places or the makeshift "foyers" of makeshift associations presenting projects they want to pursue and are searching for partners whose identity they would prefer not to know. This is a neighborhood that is party to stitched-together deals of all kinds, a place where strangers are put in touch with other strangers, where individuals with no clear purpose in mind can simply get a "take" on things, garner a sense of what is going on in places beyond their immediate experience. The neighborhood hosts all-night gambling games where police, politicians, businesspeople, and thugs all show up at the table. It is a place where special prayers are offered, curses exorcised, and secrets can be both widely shared or safely stored, depending on whom you talk to.

Whatever transpires here has no direct connection to the mall next door outside a scattering of "shared personnel," who insist that the components of their "multi-tasking" have nothing to do with each other. But when a piece of knowledge is gained, an inquiry proffered or a connection made in this Karbela neighborhood, the individual involved usually says that it took place at the Ambassador. So, while it is possible to tell all kinds of stories about how each domain relates to and possibly protects the other, it is never going to be clear which does what to whom. This is not interoperable data. Trying to pin down the details of all the interventions involved is a constantly frustrating task, although it is widely known that these interventions, whatever they consist of on a point-by-point basis, travel far and wide. Perhaps it is all an urban myth. But if so, it is a myth capable of engendering weird relationships of all kinds, strange alliances seemingly impervious to contradiction.

It is precisely these "strange alliances" on which increasing numbers of residents in Jakarta come to rely. These are strange alliances that almost operate as a version of exotic financial instruments in their capacity to meld relationships among divergent experiences and materials. These are strange alliances that do not so much connote an instrumentality among defined interests so as to maximize their respective maneuverability or self-aggrandizement. Rather they are alliances undertaken often without a clear sense of what the resultant dispositions might be. For example, while the tremulous endurance of "popular" districts such as Karbela, which run like fossilized layers across the growing "rock formations" of Jakarta's expanding central business district (CBD), generates income from providing cheap accommodation, food, and services to thousands upon thousands of workers, this complementarity, while important, is not the primary reason that these neighborhoods endure.

Rather, it is the pursuit by the popular – in its particular mixtures of political clientelism, authority claims, and tactical wisdom – of some of the very logics of the CBD that consolidates an "immunity" of these territories, at least for now. In other words, constellations of actors/residents in Karbela operate as "holding companies," develop local forms of "securitization" playing with varying statuses and ambiguities of land, design "ownership," and "tenancy" systems that are then concretized laterally over a patchwork of "properties" and "residencies." Trying to identify the clear, outright ownership of a particular plot of land and the building implanted on it takes you into a nebulous web of expanding lateral connections that stymie many conventional land acquisition maneuvers undertaken by the major developers. What is particularly ironic is that some of these developers, unbeknownst to them, are part of these intricate cross-ownership structures.

Nevertheless, for an increasing number of Jakarta's residents, popular districts are being unraveled, and their residents individuated into more accountable "citizens." These are districts that historically melded different ways of life, built environments, resources, and livelihoods in a process both reflective and constitutive of intensely heterogeneous urban sensibilities and practices. The proliferation of mega-housing complexes across the region becomes a device for materializing and staging this individuation. Attention shifts from the labor-intensive management of local, interior district-level relationships to managing more diffuse circulations across the urban context. Consolidating a place of belonging, of home, shifts in favor of better anticipating and positioning oneself to be "in the right place at the right time." Such sensibilities usually produce impatience with efforts to cultivate long-term connections and, instead, generate more provisional affiliations with workplaces. Here, even the notion of the salary partially dissolves into a thicket of other amenities, rewards, and access to opportunities.

But whether this individuation plays out in terms of increased atomization, precarity, and the diminution of any form of collective life remains a question. Rather, such individuation, as well as the experiences of Karbela, suggests the potential importance of the notion of "compression" as a mode of visibility (invisibility) for how seemingly divergent components of something – a collective or a housing development, for example – might operate in conjunction with each other without necessarily showing that any such mutuality might exist.

Free Town

I have long dealt in the coming together of those who otherwise would seem to live lives apart. At various times what got conjoined might include the inconsolable, those whose suffering was interminable, or the always perspiring power brokers willing to turn their backs in their obsessions with the backside, or the doleful bureaucrat, or the activist capable of gathering up the leftovers of seemingly ruined struggles, or the street-smart thug reluctant to live up to reputations of violence, or the armies of domestic managers who see everything in the provision of the most minimal service. While their paths toward each other are often specified and formatted, there is always something that exceeds the normative dispositions of their contact.

While so much in urban life repeats the flirtations with catastrophe, and the cheap gestures of redemption, pockets of indeterminacy, rest, and care – where no one has to decide anything immediately or play their cards right away – are regenerated. Opportunities for temporary respite are passed along, as are overtures, feelers, hesitant invitations, small lures, all of which beckon residents otherwise separated by the most minimal yet stringent divides to take note of something surprising and useful when they do take note of each other.

I say this in part because I began my "urban work" taking notes back and forth to various residents of Freetown, where I spent much of my childhood. It was a kind of part-time job based on my fascination with musical innovations in how notes could be played, my early obsession with Coltrane, Coleman, Taylor, and Shepp.

I moved to Freetown seven years before Sierra Leone's official independence in 1961. But for all practical purposes the British were largely already gone. I came with an embittered, always ambivalently Communist mother who seemed to intentionally mess up the filing of her US immigration forms and who had been disowned by her Bedouin father for marrying the son of a Camorra assassin hiding out in Italian-occupied Tripoli. Both parents had jobs teaching at a Methodist school, which both my younger brother and I attended. We lived in one of a series of apartment buildings my mother's cousin had built for residents of nearby Congo Town, whose clapboard houses were beyond repair or who aspired to a more modern life beyond the patter of ghosts, heavy rains, constant rumors, and grueling local politics.

In the early days, between ages 5 and 8, outside of attending school, I largely stayed indoors, feeling neither smart nor tough enough to deal with the crowded lanes below where everything – cooking, laundering, seducing, fighting, praying – took place outdoors. As both my brother and I had been by chance born with some kind of advanced musical competence, we spent a lot of time playing the piano at a church in the back of the apartment block; the janitor always lending the keys in exchange for hiding bottles of whiskey under our beds out of sight from his fanatically teetotaling wife.

Every summer, my brother and I were sent to Detroit for the obligatory two-month visits to my mother's father, who had joined the Arab cavalcade to the automobile factories and spent the entirety of his annual two-week vacation break trying to turn us into good Muslims. Fortunately, he always fell asleep early, so my brother and I would sneak out of the house, wander out on nearby streets full of clubs and cinemas, and plan out our own eventual escape into America, where we both felt we should have been all along if only we could find a way to knock some sense into our crazy mother.

But Freetown did change for both of us, or rather despite our limitations and us. The summer of Salonean independence, I brought back Ornette Coleman's *The Shape of Jazz to Come*, which, along with Coltrane's *Giant Steps*, promised a sea change in music as eventful as the wave of new nations coming into being across West Africa. In Coleman's music there were no bars, no background. Melody wasn't overshadowed by harmony. Within the quartet – Don Cherry on trumpet, Charlie Haden on bass, Billy Higgins on drums, there was real democracy; each player could deliver the melody in his own configuration of rhythm and chord changes, make a claim to lead the way. As I mentioned earlier, Ornette would call this harmolodics, where the same notes were written in different clefs for the same or different instruments, thus modulating the sound. There didn't need to be an underpinning, a ground on which different ways of playing would be based. You could play the game in your own way as long as you recognized the tune, as long you charted out a path that everyone else could potentially follow – so, no disjuncture, antagonisms, just switches.

Of course, I didn't readily appreciate the theory at that age, but listened to the record a million times and through it found a way to wander Freetown's streets with the confidence I inexplicably felt in Detroit. I would listen to the conversations of both kids and adults around me and simply repeat and mix up the words they uttered without really changing the meaning, but at the same time opening up the possibility that they could hear or say something else with the repetition, or that someone else standing around might take a different kind of notice to what was being said by the way it was being repeated.

Then there was the matter of style and intonation. I had also brought back that same summer a copy of Baldwin's *Go Tell it on the Mountain*, and immersed myself in the story of the 14-year-old street corner preacher and styled my delivery by imagining a Southern Baptist swagger. Even though many people in Freetown regularly attended church, sometimes every day, sometimes even the Muslims, many prided themselves on not being anything like Black Americans, and here was this white boy taking up space on the street with some impoverished imitations.

People didn't know what to make of my gestures. Some got angry, some were amused, most were simply irritated, but I persisted as if this was the only way to create a pocket of both safety and engagement. After a while, people in the neighborhood simply got used to the crazy kid with a crazy mother, and a father whose diplomatic skills and exceedingly good looks were sufficient to constantly smooth over the rough spots. He really had his job cut out for him, because my brother's ploy was to sneak out to the kitchens of the big elite families and regale the staff with his versions of Hollywood show tunes played on a toy piano he got on his seventh birthday.

Eventually, neighbors would come to me asking me if I would deliver a message to a local ward leader, a pastor, a Lebanese merchant to whom money might be owed, or a school teacher, or another neighbor now acting in their capacity as a lodge leader, moneylender, mystic, or someone with army connections. I would be instructed to deliver the message largely verbatim, but to add my usual twists and improvisations on the basic melody of the message so that it could later be claimed that as a kid I had gotten it wrong, or as my reputation for distortion started to proceed me, that there was to be some leeway in what was being promised, committed, or requested.

Oftentimes I delivered handwritten notes with the sender's request that the recipient not respond in writing or, if they insisted, that I should claim that I lost it along the way. The reasons why this disjointed form of interchange took off were beyond me. I simply enjoyed the small remuneration and the structure it provided, going back and forth across different parts of the city equipped with a mission, a foreign courier that really could not be completely trusted but also someone who had no deep social connections, who didn't really have a voice of their own, simply a capacity to rearrange what others said, a cipher on the move.

After all, it was Freetown, and in a free town, one is free to say exactly what *they want.* Now the issue here would seemingly be who is the "they" and how do you tell exactly what they want? But such identification didn't seem to concern me as I remember it now. They were simply a "they." This didn't mean that I didn't already know or get to know many of the neighbors that sent me on these missions. I had at least a rough idea of their relative positions and reputations in the neighborhood, their inclinations toward bluster or laughter, their inflated or modest claims for themselves, or even the things they wished to keep from being widely known. But I just didn't concern myself with this knowledge. Every message had its own formula regardless of whether I had a sense of what they wanted to convey, and the formula was detached from contextual background. For, its only history was to switch up the delivery just slightly from whatever the message was prior to the one at hand; it was to be a self-contained system.

The same went for the recipient. It didn't matter to me who they were; they were simply another "they," a kind of generic figure, a sender-recipient becoming sender to a recipient. It was the back and forth that I paid attention to. It was how to go from here to there that I wanted to get right, and not think about the form or content of the message itself. It wasn't that I didn't recognize or care about who all of these *they* were as personalities. It wasn't that I didn't recognize them as living and breathing residents with their joys and sufferings, or their appreciation or criticism of my so-called work.

Having looked back at this time during subsequent years and my preoccupation intellectually with the possibilities of opacity and my dislike of anything with the word "transparent" in it, as well as my own long-term residencies in various domains of the Black world and the complicated racial politics of those residencies, this declination of recognition, this compression of vast differences into a single character, the *they*, was perhaps less a dismissal of the singular features of their personhood than a gesture of respect to the openness of what the exchange could entail.

At least in retrospect, this is how I spin it. This is what I would want from having acquired this history. As long as they were just *they*, there was nothing to inhabit, no measuring of the divides, the relative statuses of the participants, no tracing out of their networks, their prior or subsequent connections to each other. It was a task with its own time, detached from the ins and outs of the cacophony of calls and responses of this city weighted with so much freight and humidity. Whatever alliances the act of passing notes along pointed to, sutured, or ruptured, were to remain strange. The people and places involved could remain familiar. The relationships based on histories of familiarity, on the details of how each was ensconced in the everyday life of the city would continue to prevail. The pounding, bearing down, expiring, birthing, demanding, and supplicating – all of this would continue to characterize the uneven affordances and opportunities of Freetown. Yet this task was to be a moment of strangeness in the familiar, not as a place to be lived, occupied, settled, colonized, sustained, or endured, but whose sheer existence was to be noted, always the shape of the city to come.

With two crazy kids, and a wife increasingly involved as a labor organizer in the teachers' union, and a mother trying to reorganize the Mazzini movement in Cicero, my father seemed to make sure that the immigration problems suddenly disappeared, and by junior high school we were in Chicago where a different career in passing messages would begin in 1967. But that is another story for another time. This diversion into a biographic note is meant only to cite the purported origins of a particular methodology of an urban researcher, specializing in the conjunctions of the disconsonant, working in spaces not habitable in any clear terms.

The Spiral and the Scene of the Crime

My grandfather, Giovanni Baptiste, seemed impervious to starting again, even though his life was enacted across several continents. Alone, he was very much alone. But in his head, he was always returning to the scene of the crime, in the shadows of the Chiesa dell'Immacolata Concezione e Purificazione di Maria

45

de' nobili in Montecalvario, a killing, the husband of a woman with whom he had a child, unclaimed by both him and the husband, a virgin birth, a birth refused scale. A birth that my grandfather referred to as "the beast." The husband was purportedly an important *Camorrista* (the Neapolitan Mafia), my grandfather a pretender, orphaned at a young age from a lower bourgeois family, bringing himself up on the streets of the rough-and-tumble Quartieri Spagnoli.

He ended up a day laborer in Cicero, the self-incorporated, and, at the time, all-white township in the heart of Greater Chicago. Cicero acted as the common backyard for rackets across the city and a haven for factories needing to launder money and skirt unionization. At night, he rented out his violence to collect overdue loans, parading around in borrowed suits with cheap cigars.

As he resented the fact that my father was his mother's confidant and frequently protector, he started imposing his secrets upon me early on, secrets that were never otherwise acknowledged by other kin or associates. After all, he had inexplicably made it to America, a man with little money, few connections, having worked as a dockworker in colonial Tripoli in an escape from Naples. He kept telling me that I had to return to the scene of the crime, to find out what had happened to the child he didn't want to have anything to do with, to determine whether it was time for him to return home, whether people remembered him even though he couldn't be specific as to exactly what minds he wanted the memory of him to occupy.

Although he never earned much, had ten children to support, he constantly threw his money away, pretending to be a boss in games that already had too many bosses. My grandmother, on the other hand, with largely Mazzini (anarchist) sympathies, pulled her entire side of the family out of the Catholic Church and started a Protestant one. She pursued lost causes, such as the racial integration of this once bulwark of white homogeneity and the curtailment of municipal corruption. I rarely heard my grandparents speak to each other, and most of the words my grandfather uttered were directed to somewhere far away, certainly to no one in the present vicinity.

The center of gravity was elsewhere, and in some ways every place becomes the scene of a crime. That is perhaps what places have in common, that allow even the far away and the suppressed to have something to say about everywhere else. There is no need to deliberate about the relevance of messages carried by the wind or waves from remote corners. For, they played their part in whatever happened. The crime spreads like dark ink, creating distorted images invoked to tease out the unconscious connections to the outside long repressed. All of the containment and erasures, all of the ruined ground cannot deter a spiraling of remainders that eventually land some place, that lure the attention of those who would rather look away.

Those present, who appear to be right in front of us, may already always be somewhere else, may have abandoned ship even as their bodies register a corporeal presence. Others may have been long gone but who, nevertheless, have left traces behind that can't be erased. Our fascination with forensic evidence is the fascination with the possibility that crimes have been committed even when there is no discernible indication of them. I have been many times to the steps of the Chiesa dell'Immacolata, preferably at dusk with a spliff in hand, and all I see are the wild rides of young girls and boys on Vespas up and down the steep inclines, indifferent to whatever is in their way, even as they may recognize that there is no way out, that all martyrdom is cheap, that history has hemmed them in, but they don't care, for them there is no crime.

The anthropologist, Jason Pine (2012) has written about the notion of contact zones as a means of creating the atmosphere of Naples. He has written about the epistemological and ontological murk through which figurations of the Camorra emerge and recede. It is that murk in which multiple claims to sovereignty are made, various social strands and networks enrolled in what appears to be a "solid organization," and it is in that murk that convoluted territories of operation are marked out. Through his repetition of a popular Neapolitan expression, "who am I for you and who are you for me," he amplifies the indeterminacy of clear categorizations of what is criminal, political, informal, formal, licit, or illicit. Neapolitan history has long demonstrated ways in which multiple contestations of political power are narrated through reifying the divisions between the bourgeois and the dangerous classes and the ways in which the actual entanglements get done.

While of course there are established ways of talking about things that enable clear identifications of who people indeed are for each other, our strivings to enfold seemingly divergent practices, styles, actors, and backgrounds into enhancements of collective force and personal sovereignty tend to elide and circumvent definitive determinations. We are often full of drama, trying to reach beyond the practicalities of managing the situation at hand, reading into things much more than they are capable of revealing. We like to turn everyday life into telenovelas of exaggeration. Yet,

> truths are made by the pressure these melodramas apply to the surface of real situations. These melodramas happen in ethnographic atmospheres – in the jangle of loud melodies, jarring words, flamboyant gestures, pressing bodies, and them and me sizing each other up. These atmospheres

hover with potential, hang like a fog, or simply dissipate. They don't allow events to be followed to their completion or depletion. We make our way using the melodramatic mode of attention. And with a sliding scale of irony, we reach for personal sovereignty. (Pine 2012: 247)

Each place becomes the site of a crime, an infraction, a disavowal of prevailing moral terms, as each place slides away from precise designations and ordering. Something is disrupted in the very act of attempting to define or defend what a place is or to find one's own place within a given situation. Whatever forensic tools we might bring to the scene to examine the invisible traces of the critical event, there can be no recuperation, no returning the scene to a situation of clarity. Such recuperation would only accentuate the vulnerability of the seemingly innocuous and innocent to a transgression beyond reason.

For it is only in the transgression that we familiarize ourselves with ways of occupying a space beyond all of the imposed definitions. For the lure of place, that which is its gravitational pull, its wealth of secrets, is not located in the place itself, but rather something else besides it, ever so near, but a nearness that cannot be measured in the customary indicators of distance. After all, for some place to exist on its own as detached from any prevailing interpretive gaze, it will have to ensure that what it points to as its own singular contributions are kept far away from investigators scouring each corner for clues.

Pine talks about how people who do not know each other gauge the possibilities of having something to do with each other, and about how they locate themselves in a web of connections that doesn't stand still, that spirals out the more they attempt to feel each other out. In some way this is about finding out what the interlocutors have in common. But the historical account is not really interesting to them in its own terms, for what is more important is the things they *might* have in common, about what their relationship *might* be.

This is an investigation that begins with a specific place or set of persons but is not interested in remaining there. It is investigation more interested in the ways that a place or set of persons might reach the here and now of the people beginning to talk to each other through rituals of verifiable familiarity. Do they indeed have something in common, besides the conversation now? Do they have something in common that is sufficient to act with a sense of commonality somewhere else, some time in the future? Can references to the past spiral into something else?

So, in Pine's account:

> if you know Gigi the glassmaker, then you must also know old Luisa, his neighbor the sansara (DIY apartment broker) who's been doing his washing since his wife died. Still more, you of course would know that great pizzeria just two doors down from Gigi's shop, you know, Nennella, where they make the best capricciosa (lit. capricious, meaning pizza topped with prosciutto, mushrooms, artichokes, and olives) – No, I've never had one there, I'll only eat a margherita (named after the Savoy queen for whom it was invented upon her visit in 1889) – Well, when I want a margherita I go to a place on Piazza Sannazzaro (grinding his knuckles in his left cheek as a gesture meaning Madonna, that's good food) – The one that serves mussels? – Yeah, that one; Giorgio the pizzaiuolo is my wife's nephew – You mean the bald guy with the missing tooth? I go to him on Mondays and Tuesdays when he fixes cars – No, that's the restaurant next door – Oh yeah, yeah, I know, you're talking about Da Enzo where there's that young kid, the one whose father ... (realizing now that his interlocutor's brother-in-law is the guy who was nabbed last month for armed robbery) – Uh-huh, that's him – Oh, so then you know Elena, his girl. She works in the

handbag factory in Campanelli with my wife. She's the one who told us about the mussels. (2012: 173)

But also, at some point investigations exhaust themselves. They turn inward and eliminate everything in their way as the original crime sucks in everything around it. *Gomorrah*, the popular Italian television show about the Camorra, points to a different type of spiraling, a kind of violence, mutual indebtedness, and attachment to place that spirals out of control, where inhabitants of highly defined yet fought-for territories increasingly become ghosts.

At the end of Season 2, the only two figures left standing are the two protagonists that attempted to take each other out at the end of Season 1. One is Gennaro, son of Don Pietro, who was imprisoned, feigned dementia for years, escaped, and who then was secretly holed up in a "fake" apartment in one section of Naples trying to reconsolidate his lost power in Secondigliano by fostering divisions in the "alliance," an always makeshift collection of different crews, none of which could consolidate overarching control in his absence.

Gennaro, who miraculously survived an attempt on his life, went to Honduras to make drug connections and then established himself in Rome, always trying to avoid getting sucked back into Naples politics and the authority of his father. But he does not really become part of the Roman family, even though he marries the daughter of its chief, who then sells him out to the police, because he wants to be what he calls his own "protagonist," someone not rooted either "here nor there."

The second figure, Ciro, the guy who almost killed Gennaro, is the maniacal brains behind the "alliance," and who eventually loses both wife and young daughter to the local wars. He is the last of the alliance to still be alive, and the guy who Gennaro "lets live" after being ordered by his father to kill him, and who refused to take his revenge. Upon his defeat by a resurrected Don Pietro, Ciro realizes that he has to leave Naples, leave the scene behind. Yet, with Gennaro's complicity, Ciro kills the father, just at that point where Don Pietro re-emerges into public.

Naples, in the intensity of its obsession with locale, with blood, betrayal, passion, family, faith – the way local leaders, no matter how rich they become, continue to live in its dilapidated social housing – in the end, endures only its abandonment. Only the two figures that then are no longer there, who abandon its scale, are capable of "living with it" but not "of it," not inhabiting it, but yet able to endure "as it" in some place that is neither refuge, exile, nor death.

Chicago

Englewood, Chicago was the neighborhood of my youth. Back in the 1960s it was largely a mixed lower working-class neighborhood of detached houses, small apartments, and substantial municipal neglect. White people were leaving fast. The declining population hosted an increasing volume of vacant lots and trashed houses. But there were pockets of relative tranquility. These became spaces of temporary respite for gang leaders cum political activists overburdened with the wars engineered by dirty cops and FBI agents in the neighborhoods just to the north.

Residents set up day cares and feeding programs, alternative academies and temporary shelters. They helped kin living in the overcrowded Robert Taylor Homes in Bronzeville to find rentals. Local community development associations applied to all kinds of federal and state housing programs to stave off dereliction, but to little avail. I left long before the worst was to come, before Englewood became infamous as the icon for homicides spiraling out of control, before Cabrini Green and a host of other public housing projects were torn down, piling up surrounding neighborhoods with keenly territorialized economies now deprived of their territories.

As the city continued to pull the plug on funds for basic education and social services, as the supply chains of narcotics played fast and loose with their retinues, and as long-honed institutions of the street were undermined by incarcerating their boards of directors, Englewood was turned into a prison without walls.

Back in my time, we had "loved ones" we could rely on. While they may have worked the streets, they did so as their fathers had worked the factories, with a sense of discipline, regularity, and solidarity. From the Disciples to the Black P. Stone Nation, the street not only pursued its usual array of messy business, but was also a university campus whose students were expected to study the wisdom of the ancients, the systems of contemporary rule, the histories of "the people," and the fundamentals of revolutionary economy. As in all loosely associated collective efforts operating under and above the radar, the gangs had their frictions and fissions. But the violence, hard and heavy as it was, seemed always circumscribed, reluctantly executed. In the long contentious milieu of the Southside, those promising days when church, gang, local ward machine, Nation of Islam, community associations, and Black Panthers were stitched together as a functional quilt in a resurgent Black urban life, proved way too much for the Windy City. So, all the trumped-up charges were set in motion, all those efforts to drive wedges and stakes.

When Elijah, a "loved one" got out of Statesville Correctional Facility after doing a thirty-year stretch, he took up with his sister on South Halstead.

Back in my time, you just wouldn't imagine that the young ones out there would figure that life was all about getting their people, who they never ever really spent any time getting to know, to put a bunch of candles and flowers and big teddy bears at the place where they took the hit. It's like they figure that this is gonna be their biggest accomplishment anyway so they might as well get down to it. See back in my time, if you were properly schooled, if you said, well even though I do this thing on the street, I am gonna advance myself, well then we had the organization to give you that experience of advancement; it might have never been a straight line; it was nothing like a ladder; you might have to go around a bit, circle back, be willing to step out into the world and bide your time somewhere else, and then bring back that time, but there was indeed a sense that you was going somewhere; we were gonna rule Chicago; we were gonna make sure that this city was for us. But now look, these young ones are making sure there is no "us" left. Things have just spiraled out of control.

Les Abricots

In what could be mistaken as the shadows of the Chiesa dell'Immacolata Concezione e Purificazione di Maria, Franketienne, Jean-Claude Fignolé, and René Philoctète began writing projects in the early 1960s invoking the form of the spiral as an aesthetic. This aesthetic attempted to both "bore into" the political dread of living in Duvalier-ruled Haiti and served as a way to exceed all the trauma of Haitian post-revolutionary culture. It was as if the potential of a revolution traumatic to the rest of the world, thus "inviting" years of repression, could be lived differently in place. Unlike many of their literary compatriots, the Spiralists never left Haiti. Fignolé in fact served for several years as mayor of Les Abricots, a small fishing town in the northwest.

Their literary work avoided statements, instead opting for cultivating landscapes full of remains, full of detached details not easily integrated into any program. For, the spiral was the antithesis of articulation. The gathering up in its equilibration between centrifugal and centripetal forces is not an account, not a line of valuation, not a device that places things in a respective or respectable position.

Fignolé's two primary works of fiction, *Les Possédés de la pleine lune* and *Aube Tranquille*, center on Les Abricots, a town long considered somewhat apart from the rest of the country. In these novels the town is not so much inhabited with ghosts or spirits but multiple times, times that remain unresolved, not relegated to a distant past. Each resident embodies the ongoing reiteration of events that could still go many different ways. So, all of the turbulent phases of Haitian history – its times of slavery, revolution, terror, flourishing, and ravishing live on in the midst of and through the doubled names, complicities and peculiar struggles of the town's inhabitants in a fleshy concatenation of enduring matters of concern and singular strivings (Glover 2010).

The residents find themselves simultaneously in many space-times. The divisions of public–private–personal are continuously inverted so that the separations between secrets, memories, everyday performance, individual torments, and joys can also no longer hold. This opens up spaces of continuous encounter, confrontation, and renewal. This is not a clarification of events or a remaking of an old order, but rather a spiraling interpenetration of disjunctive chronotopes. No one is innocent since each resident is affected by and affecting of blinding bitterness, self-preservation, and dissolution. Here, every resident works with each other in oscillating waves of harmony and disharmony, no matter where they come from or how they designate themselves or are designated by others. Speech comes and goes, and no perspective is confirmed as more accurate than any other.

In these novels, Fignolé goes beyond the specificities of a vernacular capable of accounting for the historical and present realities of the Caribbean. He is interested in the specificity of mobilizing Haitian religion, politics, and vernacular as a means of saying something about a larger world, or more precisely of configuring a space without a world, something that cuts across all possible methods of demarcation and bounding.

At one and the same time, his characters are completely diminished and trapped, but also simultaneously present and productive in a space which in its details certainly remains Les Abricots, but which also encompasses spaces and times that render the town an infinite surface. The most localized events in the town derive from or impact upon pasts and futures on a wide range of sites, from transcontinental airplanes, the high seas, African cities, and imaginary Caribbean cities, mystical undergrounds, to banal European quarters. Fignolé writes, not to figure out a new place for Les Abricots in a global world, but to deploy the town and its doubled and tripled embodied citizens as a means of deferring any possible congealing of a world to situate a place within. For example, in *Les Possédés de la pleine lune*, while talking about the death of the main character, Agénor, a mysterious fisherman, and that of a double who looks just like him, the villagers account for his life in terms that know no boundary or resolution:

> Agénor didn't have any friends in Les Abricots. Has anyone known of any enemy brave enough to confront him head-on, even at night? Yes! The sevenheaded beast. Agénor always boasted that he'd chased it away! I wouldn't be surprised if it came back to avenge itself. Possible, Ti-Georges, but the village would have heard the violent noise of the

beast and its breath would have swept away the houses. That's true. But don't forget! Agénor always brought up the fact that the monster's eighty-four eyes regularly followed him during his nocturnal journeys. Hogwash, Andriss! Why was he always the only one to ever see them? Agénor was just bragging. Maybe the deed was done by Louiortesse. What? Edgard! Go on! That piece of garbage! I just don't see how. I do! Ti Georges, vengeance increased his strength tenfold. Do you really think he had any left whatsoever after the thrashing Agénor gave him? And the coffee-drinkers burst into laughter upon calling to mind that memory. They asked questions. Their answers fused together in laughter and rum. Each one of them might have been a certainty. Not one of them was the truth. (1987: 9–10)

At the very same time, Fignolé faces head-on, and with brutal directness, the intensity in which Les Abricots is immobilized in the "real world" within which it is inscribed. He wants us to know the capacity of Les Abricots to become a universal force, a platform through which past and futures are inverted. He wants us to see how worlds can be turned upside down and precluded from restitution. But he avoids any trace of apocalyptic sentiment, replacing it instead with a narrative tone that simply accounts for the way "things are" and "might be," not as a future promise, but as an adamant reminder of the simultaneity of the "many" folded into the present. At the same time, all of this does not make Les Abricots into some romantic vestige or sufficiency to come. In fact, its power as a universal deployment comes from the very fact that Fignolé makes no promises:

Les Abricots, as if anesthetized, vegetates in a benumbing misery. The days pass without compelling us to do anything, nibbling away at the time we have left to live without us paying any attention. Left to ourselves, in the depths of a helplessness that no longer has a name because it has turned into an edifying resignation, we do not know the weight of the day nor that of the hours. Time is irrelevant to us. (1987: 152–3)

It became absolutely impossible to calculate the months and the years in those regions where its ruthless breath had raged. People everywhere got used to preferring that life be calculated as the time of our submission and of our abasement. As the time of the beast. (1987: 73)

So, when we consider all of the places so intensely punished for both obvious and, at the same time, no apparent or justifiable reason, punished for the crime of their existence, punished in order to keep the crime from spiraling outward, remember that there is a crime, a crime that comes from the audacity of the poor, the oppressed, the subjugated to dare have something to say to everywhere and that is not just about the conditions of their punishment, their marginality, their oppression. The crime is that they dare start to gather up what they have, which is more than what can possibly be identified and probably not enough to go most anywhere.

But nevertheless, at least in their hearts and their minds, they move outward across distant barrios and deserts and bush, sterile and fetid landscapes, the mega and micro, covering the earth, not with their suffering, but with the care that comes from having endured nearly everything. Having never learned or been permitted to walk a straight line, and even as they seemingly move in circles, with any fortuitous destination still a million miles away, the vibrations of the movement of voice and feet fold us all in, encompass us with some faint promise of being alone no more.

3
The Mechanics of
Improvised Relations

Most of my work on cities has taken place within poor
and working-class districts in the so-called Global
South. In these districts residents often initiate particular activities, such as making markets, improving the
built environment, managing festivals, or undertaking
small entrepreneurial activities as a way of signaling,
of making visible a willingness to explore collaborations that go beyond the function of these activities
themselves. These activities become devices for finding
a proper form capable of eliciting an exchange of perspectives (Holston 1991). They explore ways of being
together that rely upon making the relationships visible
in the moment. But they also can serve as a platform
for residents to feel out the possibilities of collaboration
that are not yet and perhaps never will be visible. This is
for them a deep relationality, a process of appealing to
the possibilities of being enfolded in a larger surround
on the basis of a fundamental resource to which they
had access, i.e. the capacity to elaborate crisscrossing
relationships among themselves.

While this deep relationality may well remain as ves-
tigial, increasingly circumscribed capacities, it is likely

to become increasingly subsumed by another kind of deep relationality (Amoore and Piotukh 2015). This is the capacity to *exteriorize* intricate histories of people working with each other, deciding and thinking through things onto apparatuses of calculation and formalization (Amoore 2006, 2018; Bishop 2015; Gabrys 2014; Stiegler 2016). Determinations of *who can do what with whom under what circumstances* and what can be produced from these efforts is increasingly subject to a form of *relationship making*, taken over by integrated systems that render experiences of all kinds into *interoperable data*. That is, data that can be compared across different kinds of locations, bodies, protocols, and operations (Crandall 2010; Kitchin 2014; Leszczynski 2016; Luque-Ayala and Marvin 2015).

The politics of relation making through data then becomes a critical facet of capitalist-practiced urbanization. Urban spaces may seem replete with standardized built environments and highly formatted management technologies and systems.

Yet, the apparent homogeneity requires the work of many apparatuses, organizations, and actors capable of calibrating the volatilities of financial architecture with the specificities of a particular context. Whatever the built environment may look like, its viability depends on the cultivation of mutable social entities capable of communicating new needs, desires, and practices that *continuously* remake what it means to "inhabit" the spaces being *redeveloped* (Bratton 2016).

The prospective efficacy of any project – making a building, a company, a deal, or introducing any kind of innovation – requires taking into consideration more and more variables. What does one pay attention to? What is considered relevant or not? It becomes increasingly difficult to dismiss anything, to rule out something as not possibly relatable to a project's likely success or failure. Given the exponential increases in the number of factors considered relevant to productivity and profitability, there need to be more and more financial and political hedges against risk (Guironnet and Halbert 2014; Rouanet and Halbert 2016). These hedges require a way of visualizing and calculating how behaviors, events, personal conditions, capacities, and inclinations exert particular effects – in various combinations of variables (Bryan et al. 2015). Generating the multiplicity of such hedges, of such visualizations of the various interactive forces of an increasing number of variables thus drives the expansive production of interoperable data and a deep relationality (Muniesa 2014).

As Randy Martin (2015) points out, non-knowledge and uncertainty have been commoditized. Value is generated from the disparity between those few who have observable information and the vast majority who do not. Mitigating the risk of uncertainty, of the sheer volatility that so many factors are involved in the future disposition of any price, resource availability, or political condition gives rise to value-bearing instruments that speculate on various contingent scenarios, each embodying a shifting value in relationship to each other. Risk mitigation thus depends on the amplification of risk, a situation that makes the future actionable in the present and, more importantly, makes this "servicing of debt" – what the disposition in the present owes this future for staking its existence on it – the responsibility of everyone.

> Whereas what has been described as the economy imagines that price is the moment of resolution of difference, the derivative operates through the conditions of generalized uncertainty as a bearer of this ongoing contestation over value in which the relation between knowledge and non-knowledge is governed. ... Derivatives perform a dispossession of self and ownership. (Martin 2015: 58, 78)

Yet, according to Elisa Esposito (2013, 2016), no one can locate themselves in the future present, "ahead" of today and its constraints, because the future present does not yet exist and remains unpredictable. It is the future in the past that is marketized, and which consists of today's present along with our present future and all our attempts to anticipate it.

> This circularity is the blind spot of finance and its logic, as shown by the crisis triggered by structured finance: financial models can predict all possible future courses of the markets, except the future of finance led by models – which is the only future that later actually comes about. The web-computer does not need to know our preferences or our guidelines, it does not need to know the user's consciousness (it has no contact with the user); it simply derives patterns from previous choices of that user or of others connected with him by additional processing (profiling and the like). (Esposito 2016, webpage)

The political and organizational correlate of such operations is the consolidation of a volume capable of generating *eventualities* (Thrift 2012). Volume hedges against contingency through intensification, through amplifying a particular present condition. Volume is amassed to constitute gravitational pulls and centrifugal propulsion – a machine for generating momentum (Elden 2010, 2013; Hall and Savage 2015; Sassen 2010). Volume can be conceptualized as the intertwining of proximity and density, bodies and things tightly packed in; where, at the same time, the productivity of volume was to set things in motion – to disseminate, propagate, and disperse (McFarlane 2016; Mezzadra and Nielson 2012, 2015). The amassing of volume also requires dispossession, dispossession of livelihoods, land, ways of life, and potentiality.

When volume is consolidated to generate eventualities, it doesn't so much matter what happens. Rather the key is to *make* something happen and to make sure that, whatever does happen, one has an important role to play in it. In other words, financially driven urban development concerns the way in which built environment projects continuously take apart and recalibrate provisioning, consumption, social behavior, and need and value creation, whether any *particular event* happens as a result or not (Brenner and Schmid 2014; Wyly 2015).

This indifference to outcome as the means to make use of any outcome is in turn indifferent to the impact it has upon the majority of urban inhabitants. Here again, speculative destruction proceeds then by depending on the fraught and increasingly vulnerable everyday efforts, ethical work, cooperation, devices, and experiments of the majority who have to try and "keep things together" but do not recognize themselves in any specific form or set of rights (Bear 2015; Gago 2015). In other words, since financially driven urbanization builds things that are not intended to have clearly productive or measurable use, but instead are instruments in the bringing about of "anything whatsoever," responsibilities for ensuring viable "portfolios of use," of contexts that enable the functional inhabitation of a majority of urban residents, fall to those residents themselves. They then face the risk that these very efforts themselves become converted into financial assets – i.e. concrete and price-bearing manifestations of resilience and creativity. Efforts, ideas, striving, resources, and products simply become folded into the status of *the many* (Deleuze 1994; Viveiros de Castro 2014).

To render more and more space, things, and people subject to the eventuality of being enfolded as an all-encompassing fabric of this consolidation of capitalist-practiced urbanization requires increasingly complex constellations of actors and processes (Martin 2013). When these constellations are put together, who knows what can happen, who knows what new eventualities might take place? There will be particular probability curves that will be deemed reliable. But as Parisi (2013) points out, the more that *the many* is subject to algorithmic relations, the higher the potentiality for generating incomputable outcomes.

What is important in the concretization of this process, in the actual deliberations, projects, and envisioning of fund managers, developers, pooling institutions, and financiers of various stripes, are the ways in which *the many* becomes a kind of endgame. In other words, in cities where I work, replete with scores of apparently failed and useless projects, the objectives of these actors – reflected in how they talk about success and failure – has less to do with profitability than with enacting the capacity to bring about *something*, no matter how viable it may be in terms of prevailing notions of success and failure.

As such, it seems that urban development, at least in Jakarta where I have done most of my work in recent years, is less interested in the profitability of development projects, less interested in developing precise calculations about future scenarios. Rather, urban development reflects various attempts by shifting constellations of elite actors and often translocal entrepreneurial groupings at more modest scales to control a capacity to give rise to eventualities no matter what, no matter what shape or behavior they might assume.

Infrastructure development, then, not only constitutes a guess on where the city is "going." It also elicits the possibility of being part of a cascading and lateral chain of significations and realignments not necessarily imprinted with the weight of particular causations or history. In an overarching environment of proliferating calculation, financially driven urban development attempts to instigate a temporality "set loose" from calculation – a process of associating place, people, institutions, finance, and politics that ramifies in *many* unanticipated ways.

Perhaps there is nothing new here. From its inception, infrastructure always seemed to point to the simultaneous presence of many temporalities. It pointed to all of the actions never quite constellated as event, all of the intersections and transactions that either could have happened somewhere but didn't, or that did but didn't go anywhere specific, or didn't leave enough of a tangible trace to point back to or move on from (Larkin 2013).

Here, we might return to Ornette Coleman's notion of harmolodics, where the apparent sameness of melody played in different registers by the "democracy of the ensemble" might generate all kinds of crossovers between the inoperable and interoperable, and undermine the dictatorship of data. Subjected to a performance within an ensemble, where the majority "plays" the data melody alongside its conventional "players" – be they developers, IT companies, or smart cities – a new politics of relations may be possible.

In the following section, I will discuss the ways in which an ensemble of varied residents, moneys, authorities, management practices, and temporalities generate multiple empirical realities that are nearly impossible to scale or verify for sure (Tsing 2012, 2013). In extracting one dynamic from investigations of what happens when residents transition from largely horizontal "popular" districts to vertical housing developments, I want to illustrate here just one small example of how the majority plays calculation in ways that instigate a blurring of lines between the prescriptive and uncertain dimensions of contemporary calculation (Jensen 2015; Wagner 2011).

In these investigations, the epistemology of the vertical tower seems to be all about quantification – price per square meter, the number of inhabitants that can conceivably occupy a particular volume, the profitability derived through different streams of payment plans. Seemingly devoid of social considerations, the vertical project does allow, however, an account, a quantification of effort that gets harder to assess in the popular neighborhoods, from which many residents came, in terms of what the efforts of residents actually do. While it is possible to trace intricate assemblages of effort and material and map out complex relational webs in these neighborhoods, what does all of this popular labor actually do, how can it assume a representation that enables individual and collective deliberation?

In the vertical residential block, prices may vary depending upon how an apartment unit is used and the temporalities applied, but residents are always talking about prices as if they pointed to something tangible and stable. For, it is the talk about prices themselves, their fluctuations, the way residents hedge particular ways of paying for units, subleasing them, even trading them according to perceived advantages of location, that provides a seemingly stable medium for assessing residents' relations with each other, a matrix of comparative efforts that go into shaping the collective sense of the overall environment.

This epistemology of quantification does not, however, get rid of negotiations over the composition of residency, but can actually intensify them, given that the formats of space that are quantified, attributed particular financial and symbolic values are not readily viable in terms of an actual living within them. In many cities of the Global South, to actually inhabit the tower in a way that makes them financial and socially viable then requires an intensification of niche socialities, localized markets of exchange that are constantly being experimented with, provisionally adopted and discarded, rather than specific styles of living *with* and *together* being the components of an oscillating yet somehow integral fabric as they are in the surrounding popular neighborhoods.

The structure of the apartment complex may appear to domesticate a particular form of inhabitation, in that it is geared toward couples and small nuclear families – a modality of residence that remains largely a minority one in these contexts. Rather, multiple adaptations occur, as extended families may purchase contiguous units on a single floor or attempt to create apertures in joining apartments. These adaptations revalue the price of a "single unit," yet open them up to all kinds of varying uses and temporalities whose relationships with each other have to be continuously negotiated, even though pricing may be the surface vehicle through which these negotiations are ventured.

The precise quantification of the price of an apartment unit as an asset may thus be displaced. But the indeterminacy of value may only be apprehended in a situation where surfaces become available precisely to be quantified, within a machine of inscription that divides the vertical project into concrete spatial, prefabricated units. This, in turn, limits the kinds of subdivisions and agglomerations possible as physical and fiscal entities in contrast to the built environment of the popular, where physical structures are constantly being changed around with different discernible values being added on or subtracted. While the vertical "project" may intend to specify a particular set of outcomes, such as the cultivation of a particular standardized form of residence and resident, quantification here may not necessarily head in any specific direction, but yet prove useful as a language for operating in the dark.

Thus, if we are to deal with the expropriation of the *many* into proliferating consolidations of interoperable data deployed to bring about built environments that are largely informed by the exigency to "do something now," then we might focus on different ways of thinking about this process of "not going anywhere specific." How might it be mobilized so that consolidation is turned somewhere else? How might the epistemologies of quantification that underpin the increasingly claustrophobic spatialities of financialization contribute to a new geometry of inhabiting, one that opens up rather than forecloses the horizons of lived-in and lived-with spaces? How might such a concept, "not going anywhere specific" characterize particular ways of managing urban life, particularly among the working- and lower middle-class populations of Jakarta and Hyderabad, whose everyday existence may be less precarious than the poor but who face intense instabilities in shelter and livelihood?

Deriving Jakarta:
The Complex Tissue of the Generic Brand

In order to address this question, I borrow the notion of compression from Alexander Galloway (2014), who, in turn, has drawn upon the work of François Laruelle (2011). Here, compression is something different from its usual connotation as a loss of details, the commodification of everyday practice, a loss of knowing how to live (Stiegler 2010), or the absolute reliance upon technology in order to engage the infinite potentialities of nature. Here, Galloway talks rather about asymmetric encounters, where things operate in the same space but have no obvious discernible relationship with each other. Rather, the ground on which they are encountered and encounter each other embodies a generic orientation – a ground that has no particular definition. It is ground where things can show up in various formats without contradiction, that does not have to be realized empirically according to specific criteria but which engenders a sense of being-in-concert.

For Galloway and LaRivière (2017), compression is a mode of appearance that need not constantly "announce" itself and its networked positions. It is a mode of appearance that circumvents the imperative that everything must relate. As such, compression is not the simultaneous folding in of the powerful or the weak; it is neither one thing nor another, but, rather, a *withdrawal from distinction*.

The generic is a possibility in every imaginable form. It is never in a direct relationship with anything else. It is indifferent to what it determines. So, it cannot affix itself to particular urban forms through immediate forms of causality, reciprocity, and exchange. Irreducible to any particular instrumentality, it always shows up in "strange" ways, turns the expected into the something recognizable but always "off" and weird, like Coleman's harmolodics.

Between now and 2021, 750,000 units of new, so-called affordable housing are scheduled to appear across Jakarta. This would seem to indicate the consolidation of vertical living as the predominant form of residential life. But what does this mean?

First, the development of such mega complexes proceeds largely in a process of "hit and run." Often the land on which the complex is built has been acquired through temporary use rights. Units are usually sold prior to construction and often on a speculative basis – whereby units are resold before the project is completed to avoid property taxes and where the subsequent buyers are often brokers who then parcel out these properties through various subcontracting arrangements.

There are often many ambiguities in terms of what constitutes the unit of property or the definition of the acquired asset. Residents are often informed after the fact that property titles cannot be issued until all of the intended units of the project – such as those still waiting to be built – are sold, given the often opaque legal arrangements between the developer and owner of the land. Sometimes acquisition of an apartment unit does not include guaranteed access to the provision of water and electricity. What ensues is that in some of these complexes, given the plurality of leasing arrangements, entitling, and service contracts, residents are paying a different price each month for what are otherwise equivalent units.

As the bulk of the units on offer measure from 36 to 42 square meters, the physical space does not correspond to the size of most of the households that end up acquiring them. In other words, the prevailing imaginary presumes the occupants to be an aspirant young middle-class couple with one or two small children who will eventually proceed to move on somewhere else. But as these types of units are rapidly becoming the new norm, it is difficult to foresee where that elsewhere will be.

As mortgage systems are limited in Jakarta, acquisition itself entails a broad mobilization of finance. This includes complex reciprocal borrowing arrangements among families and affiliates, profits from collectively generated economic activities, savings groups, the diversion and laundering of illicitly obtained money, advances on rental agreements for other properties, property swaps, or amenities packages for employees. The plurality of finance applied to the acquisition of units also translates into the heterogeneity of residential compositions. Sometimes residents related through various neighborhood, institutional, or work connections will acquire entire floors in these buildings. While most buildings are prefabricated, limiting the physical adjustments that can be made, floors are indeed remade within these constraints in order to accommodate extended families.

What often ensues is the agglomeration of social differences that not only mirrors the compositions of majority districts but also, at times, exceeds them in the pluralities of household compositions at work. Given that the new environments are not contingent upon residents working out a wide range of both everyday residential and economic activities with each other, an atmosphere of anonymity prevails, reinforced by the sheer numbers of residents involved. Yet at the same time, this does not necessarily obviate opportunities for residents to pay attention to each other, to take note of each other and work out the allocation of niche spaces and the recalibration of floors and buildings to accommodate specific clusters of interests and identities.

Consider the example of Kalibata City in central Jakarta, a seemingly standard outlay of 18 high rise towers, 3,000 units, accommodating a population of nearly 30,000 people. On the surface there is almost nothing to distinguish this housing complex from the hundreds of other so-called "affordable" developments strewn across Southeast Asia. Unlike many other similar developments, however, there has been some effort in landscaping ground levels with scores of small shops, restaurants, coffee houses, and public spaces, all of which provide opportunities for both residents and outsiders to attain a sense of just how heterogeneous the make-up of the complex actually is. Part of this heterogeneity can be attributed to Kalibata's central location and proximity to a major commuter train line, which, given Jakarta's massive traffic problems, is a key factor in the population's decisions about where to locate themselves.

Even though the complex is only six years old, with most of the units having been sold before completion, it is subject to scores of varying subcontracting arrangements and layering of use rights, multiple forms of ownership, and internal local governance systems. Kalibata compresses a wide range of financial mobilizations that draw upon: individual and collective savings, speculation, extensive lateral borrowing networks, remuneration for work, favors, money in need of laundering, the pooled assets of many different kinds of associations, and barter, where, for example, land at other locations is exchanged for apartments, and subsequently, sometimes then exchanged for jobs and for access to opportunities or equipment.

Kalibata City constitutes a non-proprietary appearance of place that enables actors to "write" themselves into whatever is happening. A place where different actors can recognize something of themselves whenever they look at it. Its residential base is perhaps most exemplary of the *many* that one can find in Jakarta, where people of different incomes, religious and sexual identifications, and age groups largely live without conflict in close proximity to each other – a disposition increasingly unlikely in other parts of the city. Even as particular kinds of identities may be consolidated within specific buildings and progressively colonize blocks of floors, the ways in which the character of the public spaces across the complex changes during the course of the day points to the proliferation of niches, differentiated intersections of all kinds.

Yet all of this takes place without continuous forms of monitoring or intervention. In part, this is because the composition is no longer a collection of discernibly differentiated identities but rather provisional formulations, where residents are more or less many different things at different times depending upon who they are dealing with both inside and outside the complex. So, while such "shaky characters" can provoke intense volatility – as evidenced in the large numbers of inexplicable deaths and more diffuse strange occurrences – they rarely leave any kind of after-shock, as residents are always readjusting themselves in relationship to each other.

Take the situation of individual units in a large apartment block. They all have nominal owners even in a situation where none of them possesses outright certification guaranteeing access to the unit in perpetuity. Given the ambiguities of ownership and the rapid deterioration of infrastructure, the normative objective is to "squeeze" as much money from the units as possible. As most owners do not live in the particular complex in which their unit is purchased, the use of the unit is then brokered by various agents, who handle a varying number of apartments and eventually acquire a diverse portfolio of units to rent out according to all kinds of temporalities – from one day to multiple years and according to all kinds of different "contracts."

These portfolios are managed in ways homologous to derivatives, where implicit understandings are drawn that enable brokers to acquire various units from each other at some time in the future according to specific conditions that prevail at the time. These conditions can range from the rate of deterioration of the unit, its renovations, its floor location, going price, locational advantages in terms of access to amenities, degree of surveillance of illicit activities, availability to be used for various functions, the character of the "social atmosphere" of the building in which the unit is located, and the extent of owner supervision over the conditions of tenancy, to cite a few.

Brokers may attempt to narrow down "their holdings" to more easily managed standards and similarities around the character, conditions, and temporalities of tenancy. Others may attempt to maximize the heterogeneity of such holdings. So, there are frequent "trades," and "options," and even these implicit understandings – the right of a particular broker to acquire a particular unit at a future time – can be exchanged, optioned among brokers or, as is often the case, converted into "rights of access" to other "managerial opportunities." These opportunities might include the right to provide services and extract fees from parking lots, markets, traffic intersections, or even access to particular volumes of goods and delivery systems.

What begins as an asset – a unit in an apartment building – becomes rerouted into dispositions that exceed calculation. What starts out as a particular piece of fixed capital with an assigned yet changing measurable value is converted, through brokerage, into a series of "intensities." These intensities initially have their form in the apartment unit, but then are dispersed and entrained to other rhythms of circulation and combination whose value cannot be calculated.

Multiple apparatuses, logics, and practices of exerting "management" thus all stand by each other in ways that do not necessarily intersect. It is always difficult for actors, looking and speaking from particular positions and perspectives, to garner an overarching story for how things work or don't work. This is the case even when they are not entrenched in a particular position, but circulate among them as many Jakartans attempt to do day in and day out. There is no contradiction or collaboration for sure. There is no way to tell whether the vast array of makeshift, seemingly improvised regulatory practices are tolerated top-down or whether interventions that percolate from below seep their way as "facts on the ground" upward through apparent hierarchies of control.

It is almost impossible to tell, for example, how these networks of brokers acquire hundreds of units in a given complex, whether these brokers are working together, or whether the subsequent territories of distinct complexions and trades – from drug dealing, to food delivery, to prostitution, to the formation of Islamic associations, to the consolidation of gay-friendly buildings – are the culmination of planned deliberations on the part of gangs, parties or associations, or the incessant pushing and pulling, slippages and openings on the part of groupings whose compositions are only momentarily stable.

Whatever the case, each disposition is experienced as equally plausible. Each stands by each other in a simultaneous connection and disconnection; where the grounds of a relationship rest in their seemingly having nothing to do with each other and, concomitantly, their relative autonomy contingent on the fact that each disposition exists.

Although Kalibata clearly has a particular history of coming into existence, its subsequent proliferation of physical and managerial arrangements during the past five years raises fundamental questions about what it is. Is it subsidized housing, is it the concretization of laundered money, is it a new form of autoconstruction, is it a consortia project of local developers, or is it even part of the jurisdiction of the official local government in which it is situated? The answer to all of these questions is *both* yes and no. For, examining the operations of the complex from different analytical starting points, from different combinations of informants, and from different archives and records of transactions, all point to the presence of each of these elements. But they do not provide a clear framework through which their proportionality – the degree to which these elements are at work in their relationships with each other – can be determined.

Different kinds of money, residents, managerial practices, material readjustments, forms of ownership and tenancy may indeed encounter each other, but in an overarching atmosphere of indifference. It is difficult to work out how they all impact on each other, compressed as they are into a space where so many distinct things seem to be happening. As such, the integrity of any of these elements, their distinctiveness as objects for comparison or integration, becomes inoperable. This is not about the assemblage of hybrid urbanizations but rather a continuous proliferation of non-subsumable details incapable of being made *interoperable.*

Most residents that I talk to do not even know exactly what to call the complex. Rarely is it seen as "home" or a "base of operations." Rather, it is most frequently referred to as a "place." When asked how the complex works or does not work, even here specificity is limited, as most people will usually invoke the word *sesuatu* (something).

Many residents who do at least nominally "own" their apartments and are more or less permanent residents do recognize themselves embedded in a complex situation of details that they do not passively accept. Each building has its own, sometimes several, social media groups used to exchange information and voice complaints. A residents' committee has long been formed to take up issues with management, even as the developer has organized its own residents' group, thus setting off an interminable conflict over which groups are accorded official recognition – something the local government has avoided getting involved with. Bills are scrutinized for frequent overcharging; complaints are registered with management concerning a constant array of infrastructural and service deficiencies. Consolidated groups of residents are involved in continuous negotiations with the developer and various tiers of municipal government over attaining some final certificate of ownership and warding off the array of surcharges that are added on as part of this process.

Interviews with more "activist" residents reveal incessant preoccupation with the amassing details of everyday existence in the complex, as well as constant efforts to deal with a persistent sense of an injustice that has been committed, not just to individual owners, but also to Kalibata as a cross-section of contemporary Jakartan society. This appreciation for a sense of a common experience does not necessarily translate into a tolerance for all residents. There is, for example, particular alarm expressed by some young families regarding the preponderance of sex work in some of the buildings and the fact that their children witness the comings and goings of scantily dressed women at all hours of the night. Yet the presence of sex workers, foreign immigrants, queers, and minority ethnicities is not marshaled as evidence for the need to remove or better control this population, but rather an indication of the indifference of both developers and government to adequately provide viable living environments for *all* people in a rapidly changing Jakarta.

A major accomplishment has been the establishment of a *posyandu*, a preventive pediatric outreach program, monitoring children's health and run collectively by a group of women residents in association with the local public health department. The *posyandu* serves as a vehicle for impromptu discussions about conditions across the complex and was the platform on which a constituency has been built for the residents' committee. It acts as a vortex of local power from which women have emerged to oversee the general atmosphere of Kalibata – from monitoring the safety of its scores of small eating places, running Islamic afterschool programs, curtailing sex work and drug sales, publicizing local entrepreneurial and public service activities, and cultivating relationships with various local agencies and government services and, in doing so, maximizing the visibility of themselves as "citizens."

This self-identification as *warga* (citizens) is something that emerges from the specific conditions of living in complexes such as Kalibata. It is not something that is applied as some fully fleshed-out pre-existent notion. Residents in most of Jakarta's "popular neighborhoods" may have had some abstract notion of themselves as citizens, but it wasn't a term that was commonly applied to the nature of their experience of residing in a particular place.

But in Kalibata, this invocation of citizenship becomes a means of legitimating particular demands on various authorities that implicitly collude to circumvent responsibilities for ensuring certain stabilities in the complex. For example, the local sewage treatment system has been inoperative for over a year, resulting in raw sewage being dumped in a nearby lake despite heavy fines levied by the environmental ministry. Yet, these fines do not deter the dumping once the developer increases the bribes. In a context where many "owners," cognizant of the apparent fragility of their asset (apartment) attempt to extract as much as they can, which largely means renting to those willing to pay a premium and thus often engaged in various illicit activities, the invocation of citizenship is a means to articulate a sense of differentiation. Such invocation is a counter-claim of stability in an environment that seems to exude temporariness.

Still, the intricate layering of social relationships, and the ways in which connections are built among those of similar professions, religious orientations, and trajectories of social activism aim to exert heightened control over the complex, to chart out a concrete path of endurance. Even as families move out to the further reaches of the city with the purported aim of providing more space for their children, they group with other

78

households, both staying and leaving, to ensure that their apartments are rented out to people who intend to stay for a protracted period of time. Here, effort seems mobilized to deter anything that might detract from their units being eligible for certification. Regardless of whether these units have any real value in 10–15 years or not, these residents emphasize their entitlement to titles.

Yet, given the capacity of the complex to enfold so much of the *many* and the resultant opacity about just how this occurs, Kalibata City is widely known throughout Jakarta. It is the locus of a multitude of stories, rumors, and impressions. It is seen as something both accessible and impenetrable, a place incapable of judgment, of tying anything down to the modality of property, and thus entitlement. So, for many, the trick is to incessantly demand full recognition of the rights of ownership while at the same time acting as if it may be best if such recognition never comes.

If anything, one could look at Kalibata as the mostly "silent" contestations among various kinds of residents and lifestyles: Islamic, queer, young professionals, nascent (barely) middle-class families, immigrants, and sex workers vying for control over floors in specific buildings. So, segments and clusters emerge. But there are so many variations of people passing through, staying long, coming in and out, that it is never really clear who is who, what is what. When one begins to follow residents when they leave the complex, it is clear that the trajectories of external movement cut across a wide range of territories and institutions in Jakarta, evidence of which then loops back to the complex that can then be "mined" by others.

From WhatsApp groups formed on the basis of a wide range of historically shared experiences, such as having had the same 5th grade class or having worked at the same factory a decade ago, to short-lived thematic support groups, to those arbitrarily formed online or through chance meetings in restaurants, most residents of Kalibata, in contrast to the activism discussed before, zoom in and out of various associational experiences without having specific agendas or interests to articulate or defend. What may be important for residents, then, is less the curating of an "inside" than a collective penetration and cultivation of a larger surround; the pursuit of ways to operate in the larger urban regions that are informed by the many itineraries of others.

Here, dispossession becomes something other than simply eviction, indebtedness, or the absence of entitlement. Rather, dispossession is always enfolded into the efforts to shape some form of "strange" commonality. Yet these expenditures that risk dispossession, these proximities, feeling out of attachments, the working out of conditions to co-exist, the obligations to both extend and be indifferent to one another, and to continuously invent new terms for collaboration that need not look like it actually takes place, are the grounds of urban sociality.

Hyderabad:
Looking Out for the Ummah from the Trash

Bholakpur is a predominantly Muslim neighborhood in the Bhoiguda district of Hyderabad that once was the site of hundreds of tanneries, and now hosts roughly 1,100 plastic and metal scrap retrieval and processing operations. It is also the place where Anant Maringanti and the Hyderabad Urban Lab (HUL) have been working for many years. HUL introduced me to this district and paved the way for the following observations.

Bholakpur is situated in a former industrial area, much of which has been converted into apartments for middle-class occupants, and these newer residents exert substantial pressure to have the industries of Bholakpur shifted somewhere else. Negotiations around the terms of relocation have been going on for many years.

Labor-intensive, highly polluting small-scale industrial production crowded into a warren of narrow lanes does present a range of environmental problems, especially for the contamination of the local water supply. Available infrastructure is substantially overloaded, and while there is general agreement both inside the district and out concerning the need for relocation, the state's unilateral approach has made this difficult.

The district largely operates on the basis of an amalgam of practices that can be viewed as a "looking out for." This is a practice that resists scaling in that it seeks to constantly reposition the district in terms of long-honed complementarities among different supply chains and export markets. It takes things in and then passes them along, but never on fixed circuits of transmission. As one local broker put it, "Bholakpur is everywhere." But this doesn't mean that it can have this access to an "everywhere" from any location. The district has long cultivated itself as a place through which things pass and where local actors circulate through each other's contacts and relationships to the larger city. Given that the state views relocation as a matter of determining the appropriate scale of Bholakpur's local economies and residential patterns, the state then just doesn't really grasp what it is attempting to relocate.

This is a district that receives bulk waste material from demolition and construction sites, discarded material of all kinds from a wide range of sources and circumstances. Businesses and their workers acquire these materials largely through networks of contacts across the region, and there is intense competition among local entrepreneurs for contacts and sourcing opportunities.

Once acquired, there are outfits that simply sort through the materials, disassemble them when necessary, and pass them into supply chains that will further act on them. There are also many small fabrication workshops that specialize in specific forms of recuperation and retrofitting. Plastics processing is largely centered on old forms of grinding, where the requisite skill remains the ability to discern the particular compositions of plastic acquired and then categorized accordingly.

It is an economy that depends upon reciprocity, collaboration, dissimulation, manipulation, trust, and extortion in varying degrees and formats. The district is peppered with small restaurants that serve as "trading floors," where brokers sit throughout the day exchanging information and disinformation as to sources, prices, and conditions of materials. A hyper-attentiveness prevails, which drives this practice of "looking out for." Since every operation is inserted into multiple chains of contacts, supplies, influence, kinship networks, and downstream users, everyone must respond quickly and efficiently to opportunities. For, the rapidity and crafting of turnover are essential to recycling operations that in general must compete with cheap formal industrial production (Gidwani and Maringanti 2016).

Thus, one important aspect of "looking out for" means taking care of the capacities of all to endure, even as individuals undercut each other. So "looking out for" also means covering one's back, remaining attentive to the flow of impressions and information that is disseminated to throw one off guard. It means being attentive to the multiple potential uses of specific materials and how to fit them into a plurality of distribution streams. In other words, it means paying attention to how materials are to be engaged in a way that both maximizes their value but also minimizes the amount of labor and refurbishing required. It means learning about changes in the production process, how new processing technologies, almost always deployed elsewhere, impact on the revaluation, eligibility, and necessary formatting of materials. For example, as new forms of textile production change the kinds of filaments that are required, prior impediments on moving plastics along because of color differences no longer apply.

As tanneries voluntarily shifted their operations to other areas, owners of the plots on which they were situated turned them over to their workers, who in turn subcontracted them to a different set of actors who then developed a local retail market specializing in cheap children's clothing. This market attracts customers from near and far. It draws upon local labor, such as women and children, who couldn't easily fit into other economic activities. As the state now demands the relocation of this market as well, the tannery workers, to whom the original owners leased the use of this land, collectively insist that relocation does not involve just the market itself, but provisions of accommodation for all of the small retailers and laborers who work for it.

Each of the predominant sectors – scrap metal, plastic, rawhide and tannery – maintains a different position around the terms of relocation, as might be expected. Yet in these negotiations, actors from each sector refuse to agree to specific plans unless all others do so as well. Thus, they maintain a single voice in relationships between the district and the larger political and administrative worlds with whom they have to deal.

Where volume continues to be a critical consideration, in Bholakpur what is more important is how the district itself and all of its simultaneously competing and collaborating components are situated in the constant passing through and passing along of materials. The important thing is how to sustain the multiple ways in which the district can act as a gravitational force that pulls materials to it through various means of acquisition and also how these materials can be rapidly dispersed, moved along. As such, volume is then re-particularized and acted upon in order to multiply the number of potential users.

Not surprisingly, in an area where contestations over the terms of its continued existence intensify, Bholakpur has witnessed the entry of many different Islamic welfare associations trying to cultivate particular constituencies. Money remitted from residents, who have over the years set up small businesses in the Gulf, rebuilt the historic Masjid Jamia as a major symbolic gesture in efforts to focus the deliberations concerning the future of Bholakpur on Muslim values. These are values that are constantly being struggled with in the performance of an economy that requires many "bad" practices.

The local councilor elected to the Hyderabad Municipal Corporation is constantly barraged by groups of women, some clearly primed by different political organizations in the area, complaining about interminable problems with water supply and quality. A more secular-oriented political party, now competing for Muslim voters in an attempt to break the hold of the All India Majlis-e-Ittehad-ul Muslimeen on this constituency, points out long-term neglect of basic services and environmental issues. Local youth are being drawn into Salafist study groups to the dismay of the older generation.

The tanneries had already been gone when a serious outbreak of *E. coli* infections hit the area in 2009, killing 19 people. This incident reinvigorated the state's long-simmering sentiment to rid the area of "pollution," a barely couched reference to the area's largely Muslim population. At first, there seemed to be a clear narrative about how this incident took place: Daily workers in the tanneries had largely gone into other occupations or left Bholakpur altogether, as new residents entered to fill low-level jobs in plastics and metal. A residual trade in rawhides, however, remained, where animal skins are cleaned and dried and then sent on to the big tanneries in Chennai. But in general, leatherwork had become increasingly impractical given the delicate timing involved in transforming skins into suitable leather and the increased Chinese domination of this sector. Yet, numerous artisans remained stuck with this trade, as well as the largely poor Hindu workers they employed, who then saw in this health crisis an opportunity to try to draw attention to their situation from larger Hindu associations.

The Leather Workers Union remains a powerful association in the district, having little to do with leather, but rather with their administration of two large schools and several medical clinics. They requested assistance from the government to either help transition workers in the remaining rawhide trade into new employment or, if this sector was to be relocated elsewhere, to identify a site that facilitated the integration of the rawhide trade into other aspects of the processing of animals.

The state responded by cutting off the electricity to the district in the hope that this would put pressure on the emerging plastics sector, dependent upon electricity for their grinders, to get rid of rawhide traders. In response, and through the networks associated with their educational missions, the union approached the widow of an ex-governor to appeal to the present one. Given that favors were owed, the woman expressed her commitment to supporting the residents of Bholakpur, and the electricity was restored.

Clearly a health crisis had occurred, and several community workers were assigned to take water samples. It seemed as if some of the gore still attached to the animal skins was washed down drains and found its way as a contaminant into the water supply. However, when curious research geologists took soil samples in the area, they found large amounts of trace heavy metals, which would seemingly make it improbable for *E. coli* to survive. So, it remains unclear to this day what exactly killed the 19 people. All of this simply obscures the fact that water and sewage infrastructure have been severely deteriorating over the years and need to be completely reconstructed. The municipal corporation, however, is unwilling to provide anything more than palliative measures, again pushing the need for relocation on environmental grounds. But they are reluctant to make substantial investments in this process unless the value now inherent in Bholakpur's land can be more profitably unlocked.

Several years ago, the municipal corporation gathered some 300 registered plastic scrap dealers to continue negotiations. But an additional 300 unregistered scrap dealers also attended the meeting and requested relocation, having the support of both registered dealers and the Leather Workers Union. Eventually, the state lost interest in trying to work out a viable relocation deal. By 2012, lacking operational space, dealers extended their houses into the street as far as their consciences would permit. Someone would extend their building by 2 meters, perhaps then the neighbor by 3. Collectively they create a situation of near-gridlock; they are stuck and can't go back, further overtaxing the severely depleted infrastructure, making circulation even more difficult, and raising tensions about overcrowded conditions (Maringanti, pers. com.).

But this tension incites demands for data from many quarters, whether it comes from now wealthy businessmen in Chennai with their big tanneries and who still own property in Bholakpur, or from various state planning institutions, or prospective external investors. Local entrepreneurs respond to the state's indifference to their demands about and participation in the relocation process by expanding their physical work plants in ways that require labor-intensive negotiations about governing access to incoming and outgoing materials, and calibrating "rights of way." All of this consumes energy and political dexterity for limited improvements. But all of these extractions of information and intricate negotiations create a constant churn that keeps the district open for the initiatives of residents no matter how much they seem to be "parting ways."

These tensions and negotiations draw attention to local entrepreneurs in ways that they cannot completely control, but which nevertheless they have had a major hand in shaping. This is a district of fine tuned balances, not overt collective organization. There are patronage systems that have had to be refigured so many times that whatever clarity they provided in terms of who runs things or who is indebted to whom has long dissipated. No one can exert too much pressure on anyone else. Despite apparently sitting it out, awaiting a suitable relocation deal, almost every trader is already part of a mesh of sites elsewhere.

For, the incessant negotiations, rumormongering, reciprocities, and manipulations evident in both the day-to-day running of the local trades and maneuvering the complex spatial arrangements that have ensued in the past five years, also generate a circuit of information about what is taking place across the urban region. As this region expands, so do the very sectors with which Bholakpur is involved. So, residents try to find ways to cultivate these elsewheres, to get a foot in the door, and to find opportunities to take control. Additionally, many residents sit on large chunks of land at Hyderabad's periphery that could eventually be agglomerated into shopping or fabrication complexes if these parcels had good access to main roads.

Here, too, the development of any concrete opportunity entails how one manages relationships with people who have many stakes. In many respects, residents of Bholakpur have already relocated, but at the same time refuse the collective visibility of all of these partial relocations in order to maintain the endurance of a Bholakpur that somehow exists beyond or beside scale. Bholakpur is something that is already gone, but in its departure intensifies the power of what remains – not as leftovers but as some force difficult to identify or contain.

Yet, there is a continuous ebb and flow of "looking out for," where residents, workers, and businesspersons point their attention to something beyond the local conundrums that threatens to swallow them. They, like the materials they work with, position themselves as part of multiple streams, chains of passing things along, as evidenced in the confidence they display about how it doesn't matter if their particular livelihood doesn't work out in its present form. For, they are capable of doing something else. They always point to the way in which their daily routines are always about the performance of *something else besides*, right next to the task at hand; something that also has to be paid attention to. This, for them, is their sense of the Ummah, of the larger Muslim community, not as a specific place to inhabit, but something that goes beyond scale, which cannot be scaled, like darkness, never clearly growing or receding.

4
Inscribing Sociality in the Dark: The Pragmatics of a Legible Home

Triple Darkness

In Surah az-Zumar (39), we read that Allah "created you from a single being, then made its mate of the same (kind). And He sent down for you eight of the cattle in pairs. He creates you in the wombs of your mothers – creation after creation – in triple darkness. That is Allāh, your Lord; His is the kingdom."

This verse has been subject to many interpretations and used for many purposes, and so I simply join as a participant in this stream of exegesis, part of a community, as Alphonso Lingis (1994) would say, that has nothing in common. For this surah, I think, indeed points to the notion of a community with nothing in common. If a "world" for "humanity" has largely been constructed by rendering it uninhabitable for those who have been stripped of their humanity when they may not have desired or conceived of themselves as human in the first place, then that world can neither be redeemed by the practices of those who have endured without it, for they offer only the hastening of the end they have already experienced, nor can that world remake itself without those very practices.

This conundrum – not being able to turn to those who have been the subjects of abjection nor to disavow their possibility of "inheriting the earth" – is the grounds of creation in darkness. It is not a matter of simply "handing over the keys" to the oppressed. For, they have already (been) driven off. It is not a matter of starting over, here or somewhere else, or of evacuating the sense of humanity altogether in arriving at the Singularity. Darkness is both condition and cover, and under the cover of darkness emerge forms of "rogue care" and strange alliances, inexplicable and provisional, a trinity, then, of darkness.

Conventional interpretations point to largely spatial distinctions of darkness, of a world created from darkness, of individuals whose initial period of gestation takes place in the darkness of the womb, and whose future life trajectories are subject to the darkness of uncertainty. These interpretations center on the will of Allah whose contents remain unknown, as do the processes of deliberation, if any, which determined that will. For the individual who lives, who may seek to live a life according to all that has been specified by her creator, there is both the certainty of redemption but also the knowledge that any final judgment is not hers to make.

Other instances of exegesis have emphasized the internal subversion of this very process, where triple darkness refers to a process of continuous invention that may rest ultimately in the authority of Allah, but whose creations remain unknown to everyone. Here, Allah is simply the power of the contingent beyond anticipation or calculation, or beyond the sovereign decision. If you are created from a single being, then is this the same for the fabrication of the "mate"? The grounding of the relationship, then, of self and other remains in the dark. Self and other seem to fall away from each other. The surah tells the basics, but leaves the details somewhere else.

In African American eschatological traditions, this verse has often been viewed as a reminder of both the curse and the potentials of the abruption of genealogy. Slavery was a brutal cut in the connection of a people from their land, culture, and capacity to institutionalize their version of humanity (or a version without it), a people whose "darkness" threw them into a state of darkness, of separation and condemnation. It compelled their need to reinvent themselves without the certainty of cultural coherence, of the dark remaking a version of humanity in the dark. In doing so, through long periods of suffering, struggle, solidarity, and improvisation, all of the historical narratives that explained how things came about and how the world was made were upended. Those that were slaves consigned these narratives to darkness

So, while the womb may be the signifier of the possibility of the trace, of tracing where people have come from and what such antecedence may mean as a legacy to the future, genealogy largely operates in the dark. Nothing has to be what it seems to be. All places of anchorage and inhabitation, all domains from which to start a story of things are unsettled; there is nothing definitively there to ensure anything but a "middle passage."

Triple darkness is of course a conceptual imposition. For how does one see and experience supposedly distinct levels of darkness; doesn't it all become a blur? The blackness of black, as the constituent of darkness, destabilizes the very notion of the human who might perceive it and thus can be experienced only as an object detached from any social implication.

Rather, the blackness of black is a supplement on the run from a fundamental relationship of the social, a relationship between self and other that wavers between denigration and indifferent detachment. At first, blackness may seem to be a supplement that bites at the bit of any frame (Mbembe 2017). It is, as Fred Moten (2008: 26) puts it, "a transplanted organ, always eliciting rejection." But perhaps, David Marriot, discussing Fanon, puts it more precisely when he says

> the thing that blackness is is not – and accordingly, our relation to it – the mark of a rupture which is both exterior and radically intimate, an abyss which is situated at the limit of judgment, thought, and desire: a monstrance without center or end ... blackness is defined not by its exorbitance, nor by its censorship, but by the way that it is always imaginarily misrecognized as a limit-work, rather than what, on the contrary, makes it so singular and disturbing as the unnamable event of an infinite postponement. (2016: 9)

As Fanon (1967) points out, it is something always misrecognized, but without any ontological definitiveness that might provide the evidence of an equally definitive resistance to any of these misrecognitions. Operations in the dark.

As the surah indicates, everyone was created from a single being but then made a mate of a same kind. But why a mate? What does this mate do? What is this same kind, and why was this supplement necessary anyway? It is the incessant restlessness of the made object, the mate, which can neither be inert nor fully on its own but yet finds itself always on the run, that keeps these questions from ever being resolved. For that made object slips on the run, never getting away but getting up and down, on and off the merry-go-round of the conundrum as to whether the practices that call one into being, into being a subject, presume the existence of that single being, that "real subject" or not. As Alessandra Raengo puts it, "black objects do not vibrate of a vitality the subject has agreed to grant them but rather agitate from within, thus exposing, in return, the subject's longing for and dependency upon the vibrancy of an object it has willed into objecthood in the first place" (2016: 259).

Throughout this book I have tried to convey a sense of the urban as uninhabitable. This is not intended as a totalizing conception of urban life, but rather to identify within it spaces and times, which in their inability to be precisely measured or scaled, where the vectors of here and there, now and then are largely undistinguishable, provide *rhythms* of endurance. I emphasize the notion of rhythm since this is not an endurance attached to particular conditions or place – such as to endure the present, or to endure the Anthropocene. Rather, cities and other manifestations of urbanization afford a certain resourcefulness as a floating topography, a means of associating and intersecting that is neither stabilized nor developed, but always moving on, even in highly circumscribed spaces. While so many forces are at work to make habitation impossible or nearly impossible in many urban contexts, I invoke the uninhabitable to point to practices of *living-with* the urban – and all of its intensifications, extension, ambiguities, and apocalyptic implications – as something strange, seemingly impermeable to calculation or figuring.

People have to find themselves somewhere, but also know how to get lost fast. They have to secure and build, but also refuse the specificities of any construction, self or otherwise, and act as if they belong anywhere and thus govern that absence of inhabitation. In Delhi, full of struggles and sufferings of people trying to find a place to live, to avoid expulsion, to survive through the extinguishing of so many things of value, the city in part endures through the absence of a world. In its juxtapositions and jarring frictions, there is not an inhabitable city, despite all the efforts to render it "world-class" and "smart." In many respects, Delhi stubbornly holds on to its constant demise, and in doing so, and despite every intention to suppress it, creates the cover of darkness and the opportunities for rogue care.

Subtracting the Darkness

I had been coming to this spot for days simply to watch, and no one took notice, except one guy who said he had seen me over the past days and wondered what I was doing there. So, we got to know each other a little bit, enough to learn that the guy had some special talents, and over the course of several weeks I would hear more precisely what these talents were about.

So, Shahid Ahmed emerges from the vegetable market off Brahampuri Road in New Seelampur with four large sacks of onions slung over his back and quickly dumps them in the back of his motorized three-wheel cart and sets off to deliver them to a restaurant a few kilometers away in Jafrabad. There are thousands of people in this area of Delhi engaged in the same occupation, but perhaps not so many who are able to anticipate what they will encounter en route with such comprehensive accuracy. At first, I was reasonably incredulous about Shahid's claims to be able to detail all of the small incidental events that he would pass through on the way to the many destinations he had to cover during the course of the day. For example, on Street 15 near the Cheap Emporium, he would rightly predict that there would be a minor accident involving a rickshaw and an unattentive pedestrian or that by Markazi Chowk there would be an argument among some tenants and owners that would spill out onto the street resulting in slowed traffic for over an hour. These predictions were made well in advance of their eventual confirmation.

The point of this apparent clairvoyance was not so much to predict a future for its own sake, but rather as a means for Shahid to decide how to traverse his rounds most efficiently and with the greatest speed. He didn't work for a company; he owned his own vehicle and built up a reputation for timely deliveries managed through SMS or WhatsApp on his cellphone. Most of his work entailed orders that would come up at the last moment, when a business unexpectedly ran out of something or had to get something somewhere in a hurry. Many of his customers were responding to an unexpected opportunity, when a task or an order broke down somewhere else, and in order to do the job they needed some additional tools or supplies.

In a world of exigencies Shahid also had the capacity to stagger and readjust the temporalities of delivery. He might already be on his way to a particular destination when a call or text would come indicating a higher degree of urgency, usually at place in closer proximity than where he was headed. So, over the years he had set up a series of temporary in-transit storage depots with friends and associates who had a workshop, shed, or a spot under the freeway or in the courtyard of a mosque; some place where he could leave things for usually less than an hour if the original request was not pressing. The capacity to take on additional complexity thus required a capacity to reduce it in other areas. The task was to foresee all of those occurrences that might result in delays.

Of course, he did not need to be some exorbitant soothsayer in order to know how to read the patterns of traffic flows at different times of day, all of the lulls and surges that accompany school schedules, factory shifts, and commutes, or the probability of disruptions at precarious intersections, roads saturated with commerce, and the haphazard improvised layouts of much of the surrounding built environment. At any given moment, it is also possible for someone possessing Shahid's acquired familiarity with all of the different approaches to any specific location to feel out a prevailing atmosphere, sense a tension in the air, a more frenetic pace of movement, or a calm before the storm. A heightened capacity for prediction is immanent in such repetitive immersions. Yet, no matter how familiar a driver is with all of the mathematical permutations of possible routing, all of the thickening of chokepoints and the sieves of back alleys, or all of the possible triggers for slowdowns and interruptions, unanticipated events can always crop up, events that are not so strange in retrospect but whose occurrence could of course not be foreseen.

Shahid's apparent capacity in this regard provided him an almost miraculous advantage to guarantee precise delivery times without having to waste energy inventing excuses. While those placing the orders were always relieved with the promptness of Shahid's deliveries, I also suspected that they were also somewhat disappointed, sometimes even alarmed, by such efficiency. Perhaps this was because they were looking for an excuse to dock the delivery price or assumed that punctuality in Delhi was an impossibility and then concluded, rightly in Shahid's case, that some supernatural powers must be involved. Yet regardless of this sentiment, they almost never failed to retain Shahid for future deliveries, and simply became willing participants in promoting his reputation far and wide.

Shahid claimed the ability to coax events from the darkness of an unknown future, to see in his mind the unfolding of scenarios before they actually transpired. But for Shahid, this capacity was incidental to something else that he valued much more. This was his ability to sense what he calls "the other side," a side that would never emerge as a distinct thing but yet remain somehow omnipresent in all that did take place. For what Shahid valued was a capacity that could never be confirmed, that was simply his to ascertain and experience. Whereas foreseeing what was about to take place could always be confirmed by whether or not that which was foreseen actually did occur, Shahid's other visions remained stubbornly outside of any verification.

For what was more important for Shahid was his professed ability to see an entire social world submerged in darkness, a world that could never be subjected to empirical validation. We all might sense that an entire choreography of social relationships takes place that cannot be adequately accounted for by the available expository vernaculars. We might believe that all kinds of strange occurrences and alliances are operative day after day, something that goes beyond the common invocations of big persons manipulating events behind the scenes or the work of djinns.

But what Shahid claimed was not so much to know all of those forces shrouded in mystery, secreted behind the limitations of ordinary awareness, but rather entire configurations of social life that most likely would never emerge from darkness. Here, there was an entire world of social interchange, transformations, couplings, and proximities that never quite make it to the outside, to the "real world." At the same time, for Shahid, this "real world" was the very door, the very materiality of the darkness in which was submerged a society free from all of the usual conventions of recognition. It wasn't that he gazed into some different space or retreated to his dreams, or looked to the heavens above. Rather, his entire surrounds were the tissue of this darkness. Yet, this tissue was only a surface without depth. It wasn't that the surface was the skein, protector, or extrusion of some secreted cause. For, as Shahid explained, what we see together is thoroughly detached from that which remains in the dark. In fact, that surface, he says, is always shifting sands of detail, with nothing holding it together, which is why the literacy he develops from his occupation, from his constant traversing the eastern districts of Delhi, is, for him, never sufficient to how he aspires to live the future.

I ask what good all of this does; what seeing the social vitality of the darkness actually accomplishes in his life. These are questions he shrugs off, that he sees as irrelevant to his actual experiences. For him, what he foresees in advance is not then construed as a reality that has been pre-determined; it isn't that he senses something that has been inscribed in advance and that he simply gets the jump on everyone else in an advanced preview. Instead, the immersion in the darkness he describes convinces him that what does occur need not have happened, that in fact, there might be things taking place right now that are not simply not seen or experienced, things not necessarily related to what does take place, but in their simultaneity posit unanswerable queries as to whether or not what indeed is transpiring is the only thing going on. For him, this is the time of the earth far removed from any world.

While he was always adamant that there were no mediations between what was actually foreseen and what could never be foreseen in his realms of dark navigation, it was through Shahid that I learned of a small initiative underway in New Seelampur to bring some of the potentials of these dark configurations into the ordinary realities of its residents. It was through Shahid that I met the son of the restaurant owner in Jafrabad who just happened to be there that day visiting his parents and helped take a sack of onions into the kitchen. It was this son, Nuri, who was involved in trying to find ways to activate a dynamic Islamic practice in New Seelampur that might spark more confidence for its residents – small entrepreneurs – to try to care for each other in a different kind of way, something he did with his friends, Malik, Sabir, Amina, Latifa, and Nabi.

I am not by any means an expert on Delhi. Most of what I know comes from brilliant colleagues such as Gautam Bhan, Partha Mukhopadhyay, Anant Maringanti, and Tripta Chandola. I have never engaged in prolonged periods of residence or work there. But it is this chance encounter with Shahid and Nuri that has instigated this effort to foreground the small ways in which a working-class district in Delhi, New Seelampur, attempts to circumvent being stuck in a world where it does not seem to count much for anything.

Delhi is a vast agglomeration and disjunction of heterogeneous elements, overlaps, mutant entities, and highly standardized and formatted zones of administration. Although it is possible to narrate many intricate histories of the dispositions of Delhi – and indeed the urban scholarship on the metropolitan region is some of the best in existence – there remains some mystery as to why Delhi is so unable to "complete" itself as some kind of coherent urban world. In other words, a mystery remains as to why the urban region remains an intensive contiguity of apparent disparities, whose connective tissue often is more spontaneously generated than being an object of planning and administration. That said, and as Sanjay Srivastava (2014) points out, the lives and places of the city are thoroughly entangled with each other as the city reaches for ever-new, ever-elusive manifestations of coherence.

"A Backward Muslim Area"

In Delhi, calling a place a "backward Muslim area" is a familiar means of disqualification. By applying it to a particular location, everything then appears to be explained.

The areas east of the old city, known as the trans-Yamuna, are anchored historically by the districts of Old Seelampur, New Seelampur, Welcome Colony, Jafrabad, and Janta Colony. These are old resettlement colonies originally housing people displaced from Yamuna Bazar, Dilli Gate, Turkman Gate, Daryaganj, and the Ballimaran areas of the old city during the Emergency of 1975. Initially, the Seelampur area was developed in the early 1960s when 80-square-yard plots were allocated for self-construction. But many of the displaced initial residents could not afford the monthly fee for the land or could only build tentative structures. Many then preferred to sell the land on parallel markets and return to the inner city.

This maneuver prompted a surge of squatting on government land for those hoping that any subsequent relocation could also generate further income. On paper, a strict code of eligibility for relocation was implemented but proved impossible to manage. As a result, 400 tenements were built in Welcome Colony – a project quickly abandoned in favor of distributing 25-square-yard plots. In contrast to the original inhabitants, a large proportion of the present population are migrants from Bihar and Uttar Pradesh.

From the inception, the various starts and stops, as well as the elaboration of a spatial layout that includes formal grids and pipelines and convoluted, spiraling improvisations, are the products of political manipulations, of attempts to undercut and cultivate particular electoral constituencies. In approximately 30 percent of cases, land allocation was made official only when prospective women residents were forced to acquire sterilization certificates. The 1992 destruction of the Babri Masjid in Ayodhya radically restructured the demographic composition of the district, turning religiously mixed communities into much more segregated ones (Tarlo 2001).

From the outset, Seelampur was characterized as impoverished and dysfunctional. This attribution neglected the systematic ways in which some residents, usually not part of the original resettlement process but rather people who acquired property on various submarkets, created an elaborate factory floor built across hundreds of small independent units. These residents engaged in frequent struggles with state authorities over their efforts to upscale industrial production. Also facing limitations on developing plants in formally designated industrial zones, they sought to upscale production through the articulation of lanes that then came to host both residential and manufacturing functions.

Through this spatializing of manufactures, and spawning of heterogeneous specializations, this manufacturing floor, depending upon new streams of migrant labor, sought to manage more advantageous positions within commodity streams, largely through an expanding capacity to address niche markets. As such, what is referred to as Seelampur does not necessarily correspond to its designated administrative boundaries but to a varied topography of roads, sites, neighborhoods, and infrastructures that fall within the same broad geographic area but which are developed differentially in order to generate a multivalent series of advantages, costs, capacities and divisions of labor that are not easily governed and often must find fairly rigid frameworks of coordination in order to be held together. As Solomon Benjamin puts it, a firm drawing copper wire from a thicker gauge to a thinner one does not require as high a level of infrastructure, say, as one coating those wires with PVC, or a firm that enamels the finished copper wire for motor winding. Similarly, a small trading outlet selling raw stock of PVC pellets compound (to the insulating firms) requires not high infrastructure but "market access" on a street corner. (2005: 252)

Since access to the level of infrastructure impacts land prices, firms often distribute their operations across different locations to minimize the sunk costs of capital investment. It is the ability of a district to have both expensive and cheap areas in close physical proximity that allows for the networking of firms to take place.

That said, Seelampur experiences a poverty and income disparity rate greater than that of Delhi as a whole. It is plagued by poor infrastructural conditions, where in an intensely vertical urbanized setting, nearly a quarter of households have no indoor plumbing of any kind, and where open drainage prevails, garbage collection is scant, and where localities have to mobilize inordinate political capital in order to attain even the semblance of adequate maintenance and repair. Police implicitly encourage drug trafficking. The persistence of caste stratification within Muslim districts often impedes the capacities of Muslims to overturn or branch out from constrictive economic relationships in specific sectors (Gayer and Jaffrelot 2012).

For example, the Gandhinagar Market in East Delhi district is one of the largest outlets for clothing, particularly jeans, in Asia. The actual market is a vast network of contractors, subcontractors, master tailors, tailors, threadworkers, *kaajwalas* (buttonhole makers), and button fixers. Stitching, washing and dyeing units are spread across Seelampur, Subhash Park, Welcome Colony, Jafrabad, and Mustafabad areas of the north-east. The production of jeans takes place across a fragmented landscape of small workshops, and the market outlet at the physical site of Gandhingar then represents the culmination of a complex manufacturing process. For, each merchant-manufacturer in this market retains their own master tailors, contractors, and stitching units exclusively attached to them.

A report prepared by Jamia Millia Islamia (2015) details the intricacies of this economy: The cloth originates in the states of Gujarat, Rajasthan, Uttar Pradesh, and Maharashtra. It is initially washed at high pressure in workshops largely located in Jafrabad and Welcome Colony, for which the workshop obtains roughly 3 cents (US) for every meter of denim washed. The role of the master tailor is to complete the overall layout of the design, to make sure all of the additions such as pockets, zips, and buttons will be perfectly aligned. For this, the tailor is paid less than 2 cents for each piece cut and produces on average 1,000 pieces a day, from which he must also pay at least two assistants roughly 80 cents per day. From the master tailor, the cut cloth is transferred for finishing – sewing, stitching, fixing designs at a cost of 34 cents per pair, of which labor costs absorb half.

The work is done through workshops that the contractor directly manages or is distributed through a network of household-based operations that work according to a specific allotment of orders. With roughly 5,000 pieces produced per month, contractors are able to retain six cents for every pair, from which they must cover the costs of rent, electricity, and bribes, given that most workshops are located in officially residential areas. Contractors must invest at least US$700 for sewing machines and electricity stabilizers. Additionally, contractors have to pay *kaajwalas* and button fixers.

The machine used for making *kaaj* is an expensive one, so there are very few *kaajwalas*. As such, the *kaajwalas* get work from a number of contractors, on average making 700 buttonholes a day and paid $61 per month. Then buttons must be affixed to the jeans, as well as further design work. Then jeans are transferred to largely home-based sites to remove loose threads from the trousers. The big merchants retain nearly 60 percent of the profit once the jeans are sold, largely because they are able to enforce cheap production, a hegemony cultivated over decades by largely Jain and Hindu traders. Muslims make up less than 10 percent of the merchant-manufacturers at Gandhinagar.

Entrepreneurs in Seelampur are caught in this vice of cheap labor and production costs, but are also "biting at the bit," pushing for the use of expanded affiliations of local Muslim organizations particularly to the Gulf as a way of expanding possible markets. They also try to cultivate new networks of distributors across majority-Muslim areas of the region, to expand the branding of halal to the manufacturing process of clothing even though "halal" status has little to do with the actual manufacturing process.

The Voice(s) of Islam

The voice of Islam is increasingly the voice of investment for a younger generation of residents. Enfolding certain doctrinal versions of Islam into one's vocabulary or everyday practice becomes a way of accessing finance that enables Muslims to go beyond simply being cheap manufacturers in the trans-Yamuna belt to the purveyors of their own trading circuits. For, as Ghazala Jamil points out, "the mandis in Delhi, the garments business, the spare parts and machine parts manufacturing, the scrap dealing – in all these arenas Muslims are kept in the lowest rung of the businesses due to a mix of spatial segregation, lack of credit facilities and discriminatory business practices" (2014: 54–5). Up until a few years ago, there had been only one bank in New Seelampur, Delhi's densest colony (35,000 inhabitants per square kilometer).

What Muslims lack in commercial power they have attempted to compensate for with coverage, penetrating and becoming skilled at all kinds of fabrication, recycling, and retrofitting. While spatial segregation provides a sense of protection, a shortcut to mobilizing labor and managing everyday complexity, in some areas of Seelampur opportunism outweighs these considerations. As successful manufacturers relocate their residences to the more middle-class environs just to the north in Jafrabad, some lanes of their former quarters have been opened up to low-end non-Muslim entrepreneurs in tentative experiments with new forms of income generation and to intentionally cultivate an atmosphere of heterogeneity.

This heterogeneity is not necessarily an active substance of everyday transactions but more a guise or diversion, a way of muddying the waters in the way in which particular blocks are apprehended by the outside world. In Seelampur, there had been a large lower-caste Valmiki Hindu population, which purportedly has mostly moved out. But this is a disposition that varies lane by lane, as some non-Muslim households do not have the means to go elsewhere or have dug in in terms of consolidating particular sectors of work. This work often mirrors that of their Muslim neighbors but partakes of different commercial networks so as to avoid obvious competition. Yet, at the same time, this parallelism lends support to overall sectors of fabrication, articulating the area to a wider expanse of the country and beyond.

Seelampur has also become one of Asia's largest scrapyards for electrical waste. Some back alleys are full of circuit boards, cathode ray tubes (CRTs) and wires, LEDs, capacitors, transistors and condensers, with workers taking out whatever can be recycled and sold. There is a major industry centered on making televisions out of recycled CRTs. This is perhaps the most intense concentration of urban toxicity in existence, which simultaneously instigates an imperative for the district's eventual erasure and a repulsive force that seems to keep any "rectifying" intervention far away. Here the past is broken up beyond recognition, its parts reduced to an elemental value, then projected into futures to be once again broken.

Acting Sideways: Attainments and Failures

Yet, Seelampur, new and old, draws in on itself, making denser an already thick coagulant, through an almost parasitical relationship to itself. It feeds on its proliferation of trajectories, commodity circuits, circulating bodies, and the wear and tear of its materiality to spawn one more extension. It is not an outward extension necessarily, nor a clear subdividing of what is there, but rather a crowdedness of hinges, idiosyncratic encounters, provisional incitements and engagements. These are not environs that provide a place or a habitat for fully-fledged subjects, but rather ones that both cohere and tear apart the settling of any fabric. This is a contaminated tissue, full of the grounding of entities into a rush of particulates. Like both composts and superhighways, this tissue constitutes a surface able to hold almost everything in its repetitive and improvised maneuvers, even if the things it holds are increasingly unrecognizable to each other.

So, residents live with an irreconcilable simultaneity of different forms of vision. They may not share Shahid's "gifts," but they cannot simply rest with one way of seeing things. To endure an environment so full of things and events in close proximity to each other, where time is crushed in order that it might then be dispersed across the world into new abstractions, where physical distance as a device for spacing things out is of limited use, a person must look straight ahead, filter out a limited working sensibility from what then becomes noise. But at the same time, the chaos of things incites lateral vision, the perception of detours and digressions, a profusion of images with nowhere to go except toward each other, toward an eventual extinguishing of sense, where each different facet of what is going on offers another entrance into wherever a person finds themselves now. How did we get here?, where are we going? become questions with many different answers.

The districts of Seelampur are sites of excessive energy, full of cascading surges and attenuations, speed-up and slow-down. The grinding repetitiveness of labor across small factories and workshops conceals other rhythms made up of rash experiments and investments, sudden decisions to take up different trades temporarily, retreats into distant shrines, rushes of amphetamine-extended work hours, surprise visits, and convivial exchanges that cannot find a ready conclusion. The day in and day out may resound, but it provides cover for many other itineraries. It is a matter of switching up what Ben Anderson calls the different geo-historical styles of relating to the future: "the manner through which 'the future' eventuates (as surprise, as continuity, as unpredictable, as repetition and so on)" (2017: 468).

The prevailing political game, while seeking to extract as much as it can, or to provoke time-consuming internecine disputes, doesn't know quite what to do with the power these districts generate. Residents consumed by the labor-intensive struggles to make ends meet, locked into particular social formations, territorial consolidations, and repeated compensations for deficient services, do not know quite what to do with this power. But all this self-generated energy in various instantiations of labor, leisure, devotion, and intensity (religious, convivial, political) always threatens to burn itself out without new inputs. Exhaustion sets in; energy is no longer renewable. These districts exist as intricate machines of experimentation; experimentation that often goes nowhere. But what happens when this "nowhere" becomes more costly and deadly rather than acting as an incentive of recalibration or of invigorating the willingness to try things against the apparent grain or prevailing wisdom (Bhan 2016)? So much of Seelampur, in contrast to what I have said so far, also seems to shut out the world, to close its eyes and hope all its vulnerabilities will simply disappear.

These districts also hold intimate freedoms – i.e. the passion to expend without function, the viscosity of the street and its non-intelligible utterances, gestures, and embraces. There is no social guarantor of individual integrity. On the one hand, expenditure does not accumulate social capital or debt, but on the other, it intensely aims for these same things. This simultaneous presence of dissipation and self-aggrandizement has no apparent mediation.

An urban tissue holds in place the plurality of activities and sentiments necessary for people to operate in close proximity to each other as both the sources of information, support, and that from which one is to be distinguished, inciting individualized attempts to carve out some niche. As such, it is a tissue that couples accountability and anonymity, traceable lines and unknowable intersections, reachability and imperviousness, articulation and detachment, and visibility and invisibility. There is too much going on for anyone to exert an overarching claim on controlling these districts, even though certain figures, from headmen to *maulana* to party bosses to goons loom large in people's imaginations and in delivering a territory to various electoral or urban renewal projects.

Political participation often takes place behind the scenes in the everyday transactions that residents, contractors, and workers have with each other. Hierarchies are everywhere, a certain few walk away with the bulk of the proceeds of a district's overall productivity. But the back alleys are also replete with ebbs and flows of success and failure, sudden spurts of money and uneven droughts. From mosque to mosque, bureaucracy to bureaucracy, and factory to factory, there are both official and unofficial emissaries suturing predictable and unexpected outcomes. Everything shifts to the side one way or another; it is possible for residents not to get stuck. Sideways movement, not back and forth, is the rhythm that is counted on.

At the same time, working-class districts are increasingly locked into a limited scope of maneuverability, to the reiteration of long-honed practices that sustain particular levels of livelihood and complexions of sociality. These are unable to provide platforms for great leaps, for trajectories of progressive or radical transformation that enable residents to shape the larger urban context in ways that provide enhanced justice and opportunity. There is clearly an overabundance of sentiment among residents of these working-class districts for a different kind of life, characterized by both greater consumption and less arduous working conditions. Perhaps more important is their desire for exposure and access to a wider set of experiences, experiences that do not judge them for any relative ineptness, that allow them to put their stamp on things.

The complex entanglements among household composition, entrepreneurial networks, financial reciprocities and dependencies, the dense fabric of everyday living arrangements, the profusion of tipping points, the multiplicity of risks and impulsive maneuvers, the intensive scrutiny of individual behavior coupled with the indifference largely shown to individualized needs – all proves a thick fabric difficult to alter and reweave. Residents are constantly doing something but are increasingly unsure about what that something is, what it means, and what value it has. Yet, the repetition provides the semblance of stability. It is not necessarily a precarious life. The situation one possesses is largely felt as being all right. But it also constantly points to the limit of what it can be and turn into. The attainment of stability, just this side of precarity, then becomes both security and trap.

Change is conceptualized, marketed and consumed largely in terms of alterations to the built environment. Seelampur and other dense, heterogeneously composed districts of inextricable residence, commerce, and production are difficult to endure. They are full of massive infrastructural deficits, the intermittent supplies of basic urban services, and the shortage of public institutions of all kinds. Certainly, there are no technical prohibitions from making substantial *in situ* improvements in the physical living environment.

But yet, there is something in the way in which the solidity of small attainments, the thickness of socioeconomic fabric, the weightiness of an overused physical base all intertwine that provides a surface of protection by keeping things the way they are. The intertwining of solidity, thickness, and weight embodies both the conditions of precluded transformation but also a motility that constantly heads somewhere inch by inch without specific destination, creating a sense for residents that things are moving. Complex recalibrations of things with each other do take place.

For an accelerated individuation of living and work spaces, or the re-ordering of density into larger mega-blocks designated as primarily residential, will, in a context of marked inequality, leave many residents of these areas further behind. So will the strict adherence to regulatory frameworks that specify how particular spaces are to be occupied and used or rapid transitions to being primarily service economies. There is a risk entailed in changing the built form of places like Seelampur too quickly because the life inside is not changing quickly; it doesn't know where to go, how to be different and still endure. Change for many residents means working longer hours, taking on more debt, living at a far remove from the city as the only affordable option, and having to do all this largely as individuals responsible for themselves.

So, it is not an account of the discernible conditions that renders these irregular districts "uninhabitable." Rather it is precisely because there is no discernible scale on which to work out the conundrum that these places exist as both protection and trap. It simply is not clear yet what would constitute a different kind of habitability with different roots, one that doesn't take 12–14 years from now in order to reach some clear signs of fruition, but more like 3–5; that doesn't have to wait for conditions of emergency or violent conflict in which transformation always assumes a particularly twisted "management style."

The uninhabitable is this surface outside of scale, that moves to exceed the locked-in relationship between protection and trap to foresee how Seelampur can go beyond what it is in order to be itself, an identity which is not static or complete, but indicative of a process of making anew and again.

Dominic Boyer (2017) has written of infrastructure as a gelatinous congealment of labor, cognition, materials, technicity, and politics that stores inordinate amounts of energy conventionally deployed in an always expanding latticework of connectivity, driven by fossil fuels and constitutive of a social form that buttresses the imperative of expansion. By citing infrastructure's revolutionary potential, he also explores the possible ways through which energy can be generated, held and distributed through a multiplicity of more localized assemblages, through which variously demarcated populations might more effectively participate as purveyors, users, and managers.

For Seelampur, this would mean that all the denim stitched, all the metal cabinets welded, all of the wires stripped, and circuit boards dismantled are not passed on somewhere else where the real value lies. It means extending the fabrication process, not necessarily inside Seelampur, but to a range of elsewheres, in alliances that ensure it a continued hand in the making process. Whereas tentative accommodation among confessional communities in Delhi largely operates through disproportionate access to the value extracted from the production process – as we have seen with the jeans story – the subvention of the primacy of these identities has been demonstrated in recent years in Seelampur itself, through "strange" and momentary alliances between Hindu and Muslim workers, if not necessarily contractors.

Rogue Care: An Incipient Islamic Urban Politics

Any district will have to work with its own peculiarities of identity and history in order to configure a scale without scale, to circumvent the conundrum of their existence as both protection and trap. In Seelampur, as a majority-Muslim area, actual interest in Islam is often perfunctory. Religious obligations are rigorously attended to but the thirst for learning about the religion is minimal. This is reflected in the general lack of interest on the part of families to provide their children with any formal religious training. Attempting to overcome a range of obstacles, a new generation of highly educated Seelampur residents aspires to new ways of life and occupations.

But many also flinch at the way in which the ordinariness of middle-class life in Delhi is largely being defined in Hindu nationalist terms, particularly by the ruling Bharatiya Janata Party. While middle- and upper-class Muslim colonies have developed over the past several decades, and Jafrabad, just north of New Seelampur, has experienced a boom of new upper middle-class pitched construction, many of this generation still live amongst and maintain connections with their kinship and locality networks in the older districts. But they want to do this in a different way.

In New Seelampur, the group of young Muslim professionals I mentioned earlier started to meet two years ago in the face of a seemingly minor event. They were struck by the fact that with all of the engineering and other technical skills the district possessed, these could never be mobilized to adequately repair the air conditioning at the mosque where they performed their daily prayers. Those that began meeting saw this deficiency as part of a larger tendency of skill and labor being locked into outmoded production and trade networks, into guilds and associations that kept reiterating individualized entrepreneurial responsibility rather than providing platforms for experimentation in how things were made and sold.

They recognized that the vast majority of residents in the district had a rudimentary understanding of Islam and understood their task not as extending the community's knowledge about Islam or to invigorate a more authentic or comprehensive practice of it. Rather, the task they assumed was how to translate the vernacular knowledge and words the communities did possess into an instrument to demonstrate how residents' work lives could work differently. In lives implemented across narrow margins, their idea was to expand the scope of lateral connections among workshops, storehouses, shops, transport practices, and distribution outlets in a way that provided new contexts of actualization for the everyday religiously inflected discourses that residents used with each other.

Careful not to be seen as usurping the authority of local religious figures or local political bosses, they organized small receptions with food and refreshment, where they simply presented short videos documenting different forms of everyday life in different parts of the Muslim world. They invited friends, neighbors, and other contacts so that a mix of people from different parts of the district would show up, encouraging the participation of families and individuals of all ages. The emphasis was on having a good time, of not being didactic, of not installing a particular agenda.

Participants would hesitantly discuss what they saw, and over time did so with increasing confidence, where participants themselves examined the connections between what was viewed and life in their district. The organizing group always responded to these examinations with a multiplicity of viewpoints and possible ways of doing things. For, the objective was not to build a new organization or generate a new economic development program for the district but to enable at least some of its residents to envision the possible concrete steps that could make better use of the skills they already possessed.

How could these skills be used outside of the strictures of economic organization to which they were subjected without necessarily making their position more precarious within the transaction circuits in which they were already embedded? Even as these residents worked long hours, often struggled to keep up, the idea was not to supplant their positions but to find viable ways of supplementing them by suturing together lateral connections that might generate new prototypes, craft select batches of new products that could be tested in markets outside the prevailing ones, and consider how to generate expanded markets of internal consumption based on mobilizing skill and labor to make the delivery of local urban services more efficient and cost effective.

At every juncture there were efforts to demonstrate just how all of these steps were indicative of the critical Islamic concepts of belief, faith, propriety, and propa gation that populated everyday speech. This initiative attempted to prompt participants to move across the space of the district in different ways and to think of its pathways and articulations as a series of different thresholds and possibilities of action. Most impor-tantly, it sought for residents to attend to each other, look to and for each other through a different ocular architecture.

In other words, these efforts attempted to continue building an atmosphere about what it means to be a Muslim resident, or as Alberto Corsín Jiménez and Adolfo Estalella (2013) put it, to look for each other as they look after each other. The process does not cement ties; it is not a matter of belonging or relational incor-poration into established systems of meaning. Rather, these are demonstrations of elasticity, to test out and not simply assume where the "hard" boundaries might be.

Coming Home

It was the stories and films of Shenzhen that particu-larly fascinated the participants in this experiment.

Not so much as a model, but as series of occurrences and possibilities that might be harvested, particularly since Shenzhen was largely a story about how to make unanticipated ways of urban living out of failure – the failure of state-imposed imaginaries, the failure of trying to organize life according to strict rules and parameters. Failures that, nevertheless, became successful, because failure opened up a space for multiple compensations that had to find ways of accommodating each other.

Failure indeed takes a higher toll on the ordinary. In poor and working-class areas across the South, failure was once something to be absorbed; it wasn't something clear-cut, but more of a blur. One could blur failure, move into a zone where its sting and costs could be attenuated and perhaps transformed into an incitement to try something new, again.

Muslims across the world are preoccupied with failure. They have failed to realize nearly impossible aspirations about unity, about truly merging religious guidelines into political practice and governance. They are preoccupied with the failure to free Palestine from Zionist rule. They are preoccupied with the failure to adequately protect themselves from a growing wave of discrimination, as well as their failure to establish Islam as unequivocally a religion of peace. But what was interesting for these residents of New Seelampur, fascinated with the story of Shenzhen, was the productivity of failure; that they could try small things, do things in a different way, and blur the lines of who was to be blamed if things didn't work out, to blur the lines of whether something really worked or not.

Their efforts take place in a city that has witnessed the active construction of middle-class imaginaries through the ascendance of local resident welfare committees acting in close partnership with various tiers of the state. These partnerships have worked to concretize such imaginaries among disparate districts of the city through securing spatial boundaries, supporting local entrepreneurial activities, cultivating wide-ranging networks among local activists, bureaucrats, technicians, and politicians, as well as generating various formats to promote conviviality (Srivastava 2014).

Although these assemblies in New Seelampur may seem in some respects to mirror this general trend, there are few expectations that any partnership with the state is being furthered, little sense of or aspiration to consolidate a coherent social body. This does not mean that residents here don't engage the state, in its various tiers and local manifestations. But it is an engagement where timing is everything; where interstices are opened up that enable low-level bureaucrats and technicians, in particular, to operate with sufficient autonomy and confidence to take care of different problems, such as water connections or electrical supply (Ghertner 2017). Small collaborations come and go.

So, too, do small collaborations among participants in this New Seelampur "project" come and go. Daily life is too tough for people to be weighed down with too many obligations, so everyone attempts to elicit attention, time, and cooperation through whetting curiosity, providing momentary respites from the ordinary, as well as favors and support that make the management of work and household a little bit easier. Things get fixed, but also "curtains" are pulled, as participation in the project proceeds with different rhythms.

After several months, Nuri, Malik, Sabir, Amina, Latifa, and Nabi would ask participants at the close of each gathering about what kinds of people they would wish to express themselves to, to be in contact with, to inform about their ideas and experiences. They emphasized that such a list was not simply to identify people in power from whom they wanted assistance or even recognition, but rather people they would be curious to know or to be known to.

Eventually participants would draft communiqués actually addressing these others – mostly not named as specific individuals but as types of characters – actors, metro conductors, factory owners, school principals, and so forth. As many participants were artisans, they prepared these communiqués with great flourish and style in their choice of paper and embossment. Lists were drawn putting plausible names to these characters, and each communiqué listed the number of Nuri's parents' restaurant where contact could be made, as well as an email account and Facebook page, in which they identified themselves as a new form of "co-working space in New Seelampur." Shahid was then tasked with delivering the communiqués across the city, for as time went by, the participants sought to have greater reach beyond this vicinity of the Yamuna River. Of course, as Nuri indicated, very few calls ever came in; there was no guarantee that the communiqués delivered were widely read.

But everywhere Nuri went in the district – a district that for the most part had little idea about what he and his colleagues and about a hundred residents were up to – he heard stories from others that people in their various places of work, worship, and social affiliations were talking about some strange occurrences in New Seelampur.

These small efforts do not obviate the need for more extensive political projects. Explicit connections need to be drawn between infrastructure investment and its resource efficiency, distributional effects, and the impact on the unsustainable and unjust path dependency of the operating systems of the city. This line of political reasoning opens up every single infrastructural system, land-use plan, and economic investment to close public scrutiny in terms of whether it contributes to aggregate resource efficiency and whether it deals with differential densities in a way that can foster spatial justice for all (Amin 2014).

But increasingly, states and real estate mafias and insulated elite provoke and prey off a more generalized fear of failure. There was no need for the air conditioning to fail in the mosque, but who would risk attempting to rectify the situation in front of everyone if such efforts might fail. So better let failure be a kind of default position. So this project attempted to cultivate an atmosphere where failure might not be so debilitating. For even in their own efforts, these young professionals risked failure, risked wasting their time and money in a place where everything seems stuck. But what ensued was a commitment on the part of the participants to pay attention to each other, to attend to their half-baked trials and errors, to lend confidence but not get in each other's way, to not arrive at the definitive best practice or to issue definitive judgments. In this way, they lent each other an experience of "home."

For, what is home? In Toni Morrison's short novel, *Home*, the main protagonists, brother and sister, Frank and Cee, find themselves forced to return to a home in Lotus, Georgia, they never really considered as such. Both saw themselves as exiled there as children, never really welcomed, and anxious to take any opportunity to leave. But both failed in their journeys into a larger world. Both came back wounded and close to death. For the young sister, repeatedly experimented upon and nearly killed by a racist physician obsessed with eugenics, her care was assumed by a group of elder women, each with their very different approaches to healing.

They took charge of her, gave her no leeway in terms of her adherence to a strict protocol of interventions that were not so much a composite of the individual skills or preferences of the elders but more a series of rhythmic alterations. As Cee goes up and down, as fevers come and go, each distinct intervention has its turn, finds its time of application in relationship to the others and in relationship to the responses of the body to which they are applied. What the women share is not so much a common approach but a sensibility rooted in their deep knowledge that whatever they do is situated in larger surrounds of give and take. They have an unwavering confidence in their ability to endure in an overarching environment of failure (Amin 2016). For, their blackness is worn both as knowledge that they exist in a world of darkness, but that they, themselves, are not in the dark.

Morrison describes one of the women:

> an aggressive gardener, Miss Ethel blocked or destroyed enemies and nurtured plants. Slugs curled and died under vinegar-seasoned water. Bold, confident racoons cried and ran away when their tender feet touched crushed newspaper or chicken wire placed around plants. Cornstalks safe from skunks slept in peace under paper bags. Under her care pole beans curved, then straightened to advertise their readiness. Strawberry tendrils wandered, their royal-scarlet berries shining in morning rain. Honeybees gathered to salute *Illicium* and drink the juice. Her garden was not Eden, it was so much more than that. For her the whole predatory world threated her garden, competing with its nourishment, its beauty, its benefits, and its demands. And she loved it. (2012: 130)

Here is a woman who risked failure but kept on going, knowing that she functioned in a field full of predators. So, home is not a place of safety; it is not a refuge from the world. Home is not a single orientation that roots the inhabitant in security. It is a place of operations, of a multiplicity of sentiments and practices that exert a tough love on the recipient. It is a no-nonsense urgency to submit and adhere to a wisdom that is not yours specifically, but which is nevertheless a legacy inscribed in one's very physiology – a swirling sea of marks, traces, and vernaculars, so much more than genetic. Home is a fabric of pieces, leftovers, and things discarded. It is that which all of the piecework done in Seelampur and in thousands of other districts across the world hold on to, that don't enter the commodity chains, that mostly never get used, but could. Home is always stitched together – tissue, fabric, and bodies alike. It is also not just for us to keep.

In the closing lines of the novel, Frank drags a reluctant Cee to the site of something they witnessed as children – a game where black fathers and sons had to fight each other to the death at the command of drunken white farmers. They had seen the body of the loser hurriedly buried. After the elders restored her to health, Cee joined in the common practice of quilting, of stitching together her first tissue. But in this final scene, the quilt, the tissue is sacrificed in the act of digging up the remains of that body, wrapping it, and giving it a "proper home."

5
The Politics of
Peripheral Care

Undoing Harm

What does it mean to collect evidence of harmful situations? How is that evidence constituted; how does it take hold in particular bodily experiences and for different constituencies? There seems to be little to mitigate our collective addiction to bearing witness to the repeated scenarios where life is bared. Where the identification and pursuit of one particular kind of terror devolves into a situation far worse than the initial threat posed; where all of the acts of containment ramify to set loose increasing numbers of people from viable livelihoods and relations to place.

Elite obsessions with any social movement that exemplifies an absolute unwillingness to tolerate injustice, and which may mutate into a viciousness often characteristic of such a singularity of vision, tend to lead to interventions that come to depend upon the very thing that is obsessively feared as the only way to stave off a far worse disaster. One only has to draw a line from Dakar to Djibouti, and from Mekkah to Peshawar, to understand how various and partial claims to the Muslim Ummah get converted into a global hysteria that prompts interventions that simply propagate ecological, humanitarian, and political harm that cannot be rectified.

While harm and danger may be immediately evident without the need for reflection, there are situations where harm is more diffuse and not readily discernible without innovative devices of sensing or speculative practices. These practices entail the emergence of new forms of social cooperation, capable of validating and conveying provisional bodies of evidence into actionable political instruments (Gabrys 2014, 2017). Gabrys' injunction may be an important starting point in reconsidering a politics of care when she formulates care as a "speculative mode of encounter that is differently articulated in relation to the entities and collectives that are informed through monitoring practices that attempt to evidence experiences of harm" (Gabrys 2017: 177).

What happens when specific situations or times become so saturated with toxicity, and where toxicity is ignored because paying attention to it would only mean that the money often associated with it would move elsewhere, or where the toxic is turned into a familiar, if no less lethal, companion? All of the evidence that could be marshaled in order to instigate people to get out, desist, or rebel may simply "stand by" as a silent witness to the conditions or events at hand, as well to the affected bodies – now simply appendages to the host of monitoring measures applied.

This is not to give in to disaster, but merely to recognize the surfeit of preoccupation with it that then often seems to disqualify real or feigned indifference. Where indifference is only seen as resignation on the part of those who continue to live through it, by it, and *with* it. While it is important for residents of apparent deleterious conditions to demonstrate what indeed matters to them and have recourse to converting attention into amelioration, the kinds of care and interventions that these demonstrations might instigate may at times be limited to that which makes sense only outside the lived experience of those very residents. There can be situations where indifference is just what it is – indifference; indifference to the normative expectations of how someone should react, how they should take care of things.

These are residents who then might simply be accused of false consciousness or internalizing domination. In other words, many attempts to "make things better" dismiss those who attempt to forge a kind of sense in the moment when all "common sense" seems to disappear, or who situate themselves beyond preventive care. As Musa al-Jawani, an 18-year-old thief from the infamous Gayati Mayo slum in Khartoum emphatically concludes: "I do not want a life; I do not want any trace that I was here, even though across this town, I do relish in the rumors I hear that many big men and big women simply can't believe that some of their possessions, which I resell for almost nothing, have actually disappeared, as well as any trace of the crime."

Sometimes a politics of care is a matter of concretizing new lines of connection, as Asef Bayat describes a particular poor neighborhood in Cairo during the advent of the Egyptian Revolution of 2011:

> The ashwaiyyat communities such as Imbaba housed not merely the rural, illiterate, and abject poor but also segments of the "middle-class poor" – government employees, newly married and educated couples, as well as professionals such as lawyers and teachers – who could not afford to secure housing in the formal market. The members of this class, traversing between the "middle-class" world and that of the "poor," critically linked the local struggles of their dispossessed parents, relatives, and neighbors to the world of the universities, journalism, cyberspace, associational activism, and the main streets. (2015: S37)

But as Bayat goes on to say, the hundreds of protests, strikes, collective initiatives, reclamations of space, generation of markets and street enterprises, appropriation of land and buildings engineered by the poor in the aftermath of the revolution, could not alter the larger institutional biases against the poor or the way in which the management of urban space itself is largely dedicated to ensure the insufficiency of such collective efforts.

An urban politics, then, must urgently enable the vast reservoir of vitality emanating from streets and popular districts to permeate the very infrastructure of decision making and provisioning. Whether this can be actualized or not, the possibility of such a politics entails at least the envisioning of an active *refusal of inhabitation* in its present terms, even when the making of that inhabitation in much of the South is self-generated and self-evolved by the majority of residents. If not obviously looking like refusals, many gestures of such do get made all of the time.

For surges of political affect do not always take on the recognizable vernaculars of autonomy, resistance, and freedom. Have not rhythms of endurance, as we have noted in the different discussions so far, proved more nuanced than this, more adept at working their way across various modalities of expression?

As Povinelli (2017) points out, late liberalism invests in the continuing illusion of the autonomy of objects, the contestations of defined positions, and possibilities of plural becoming. All of these are purportedly open to a wide range of possible futures, and particularly the possibility that an autonomous individuated self can, through will and skill, determine the course of particular futures. But this possibility is grounded on relegating all of that which is not oriented toward such individuation to a past that no longer has anything to say. The examples she uses center on Australian indigenous thought.

This past, then, is forcibly subjected to conditions that curtail its powers of proposition and render it, if it indeed continues in some form of recognition, as the "truth" of the past, something frozen in particular, self-contained, and completed manifestations, incapable of being anything else than what they are and always have been (Povinelli 2017). She goes on to insist,

> The illusions of our epoch are the autonomous and antagonistic. Other illusions may be better suited. Viruses, gassings, toxins – these are the names we give to manners of appearing and spreading; tactics of diverting the energies of arrangements of existence in order to extend themselves; strategies of copying, duplicating, and lying dormant even as they continually adjust to, experiment with, and test their circumstances; maneuvers to confuse and level every difference that emerges between regions while carefully taking advantage of the minutest aspects of their differentiation. (2017: 308)

So, too, the manners of appearing and extending for an urban "majority" – what we might have called auto-construction in the past – take on different modes of visibility and collective enactment. Here, I use the notion of "collective" not as a coherent entity but as something more diffracted and superpositional. The collective is a means of deploying force, of folding in discernible individual lives and things into spaces of operation that are not inhabitable in a strict sense (Caldeira 2016; Corsín Jiménez 2017). In other words, the equation that links inhabitation to the hosting of something definable and that lends definition to that which inhabits, situating it in a complex ecology of interdependency and sustainable life, is upended in an urban mathematics that simultaneously situates residents in entangled multiplicities of constraint and potential, as well as thick webs of alternating governing and arbitrariness. While a vanguard, a proletariat, or a political movement may not be simply anachronisms, it is necessary to consider the shape-shifting "bodies" of collective enactment, all of the ways in which people and things can and might operate in concert. Here, a more expansive notion of solidity might be required, solid not like flesh, but like a beat, or an amalgam of body and machine that issues beats, pulsations capable of carrying things away, in that strange vortex between being involuntarily carried away and acts of mutual carrying, *hijra*, where being-on-the-way elides any capture.

Dangerous Rehearsals

Urban landscapes are increasingly marked with the conceit of enclosure (Sevilla-Buitrago 2015), the marking of territory as the exclusive prerogative of ownership immune from articulations to larger surrounds, except those dictated by statute or the economic advantage of the owner(s). Enclosure reflects the belief in a delirious detachment, where those who exercise rights over territory can withdraw from having to negotiate with the multitude of others who exercise their own particular claims to livelihood and imagination across an urban region. Not only have evictions and displacements accelerated through a variety of mechanisms, but increasing numbers of residents have bought into the possibilities of enclosure as a normative practice, as a modality of living indicative of their worth and eligibility to be part of the city. This is the case even when their subsequent location seems to remove them far from the city's center of gravity.

From Istanbul to Beijing to Bangkok to Jakarta to São Paulo to Brooklyn, the urban core is being cleansed of its working class, lower middle class and poor populations

– its majority. From forcible evictions to seduction, from promises of a better life to harsh reminders of expendability, the majority is reconstituted at the periphery in a process of mass suburbanization (Keil 2017). As such, urban politics will largely be a peripheral politics, not only a politics at the periphery, but a politics whose practices must be divested of many of the assumptions that it derived from the primacy of "the city." The latter was a politics of self-reflecting subjects articulating futures in terms of rights and democratic participation. The periphery, on the other hand, is a compost machine processing the leftovers of city life into a mulch of strange contiguities that don't know what to make of each other, that don't know any particular interest to defend or to negotiate with.

For the question is: where is everyone going to go who are the leftovers from displaced occupancy in the urban cores, displaced either on the basis of their unseemly poverty, dangerous practices, economic calculations or embrace of a more individuated, affordable, and consumption-maximized existence? The subsequent shaping of peripheries does not neatly sort out these differentiated trajectories of exodus.

Massive outlays of affordable vertical housing for the lower middle classes are interspersed with quickly assembled catchment zones for the urban poor, all of which intersect with an assortment of industrial land, relocated factories, ruined leisure zones, waste dumps, warehouses, and the vestiges of upscale gated communities. Most of the built environment is not built to last. Large estates of small pavilions that promised home ownership and fungible assets to the wage earners are rapidly decaying and abandoned not even a decade after their completion. Populations are inserting themselves in the fuzzy interstices of no-man's-lands produced by the exigency to further separate out the deserving from the non-deserving classes, alongside and underneath various transport infrastructures, land banks, and vast arrays of industrial and commercial spaces that are neither fully operational nor depleted.

Urban populations are being culled, perhaps for reasons that have little to do with urban life per se but rather with using the reconstituting of the urban for a much larger planetary project of dismissing the majority in favor of the ongoing survival of the few. After all, the conversion of urban cores into spectacular financialized ephemera often does not work in terms of any other apparent function but incessant abstract conversion. They remain useless in any other sense. They pad portfolios designed to subsidize the end of use; a planetary program that sees no use in the ongoing existence of a majority. Despite real estate reports touting the urgency for larger volumes of commercial square footage and amenities for the rich, many projects stand nearly empty, cultivating a tolerance for emptiness.

Whereas the city was the locus for forging a generalized notion of a common humanity for which the city was to be primary evidence, this generation of vacuums in the urban core and the accelerated turnover of the material environment appears to be preparation for the abandonment of any generalized humanity. It is the locus for which the privileged can "head for the hills," "cut the natives off at the pass," and to do so without the semblance of committing a crime, since the crime is now the responsibility of all of humanity (Ruddick 2015).

As Cohen and Colebrook point out:

> Looking ahead decades, passively engineered population culling need have no overt fingerprints and presents no ethical agony for an advanced, if related, "species" – or, more accurately, a turbo charged version of what, all along, has been the species that is not one, since everything it had identified with and proprietized as archival arts,

mnemotechnologies, semio-aesthetic sensoria, and digital totalizations were, already, materialistic signifying chains neither human, explicitly, nor living as such. (2017: 140–1)

The periphery is, then, not only a particular spatializing of the urban but a receding of the very ideological basis of urban life as the great synthesizer, as the locus of cosmopolitical attainment. The periphery also recedes as a frontier. Once nascent residents could calculate the most strategic of locations, where to place themselves according to what they could afford, but also consider affordability in terms of proximity to transport or work, to the eventual growth of a particular area, or to the availability of particular services and their relative costs. Residents of the periphery not only sought a place to live but also an opportunity to design a world for themselves based on speculation about how the periphery would eventually be "filled in" and how they wanted to situate themselves accordingly.

Towards a Peripheral Political

Now the peripheries are increasingly crowded, over-run, and in many respects an urban politics begins with this crowdedness, with a situation where residents increasingly have to "take what they can get," to situate themselves as best they can in surroundings where anticipations of the future seem nearly impossible. So, a politics begins here in the dissolution of volition and unintended entrapment, where residents who have arrived on different trajectories of impetus are stuck with each other in a seemingly permanent state of the provisional.

On the surface, some of these peripheries appear ungovernable. I often visit family members living in such a periphery, Citayam, near the end of one of the commuter lines in Jakarta. It is raining and the muddy thoroughfare that runs in front of the station is grid-locked with traffic, as are all of the surrounding roads. No one moves waiting for their app-based transport, cheap buses, or motorbike taxis. The stalled buses are immediately converted into pop-up stores selling cigarettes that "fell off the truck" and Singapore lottery tickets. The crowd assembled under umbrellas in front of the station circle around land brokers who offer community trusts on former rice fields. Teachers from surrounding Islamic schools peddle brochures, while an interminable line of porters carry goods between the station and the nearby markets. Local municipal bureaucrats dispense with their offices and set up small tables under the canopies of dry goods stores spreading out in every direction from the station, attempting to enlist ingoing and outgoing passengers in various registration schemes, from health immunizations to local security campaigns.

This was once a market town serving surrounding rice fields. The area is frequently flooded and the scores of thousands of new residents and their houses and stores and vehicles have simply exacerbated the wetness. Very few roads run in a straight line and very few can really accommodate vehicles traveling in both directions. What it means to be close to the train is a calculation that changes daily. The area has become a receptacle for all kinds of projects and life circumstances. People are on the run from something, and they have imbued Citayam with fantasies of all kinds. All the political parties have descended en masse to establish branches and enroll constituencies, but few residents are interested. Nor are they interested in the populist religious vernaculars that are sweeping across the older parts of Jakarta.

It is impossible to go to work on the train without being "intercepted" with some new scheme, some new proposal for joining lots, reducing food costs by buying in bulk with others, of putting in an order from someone on their way to shop in Kuala Lumpur. These are all fly-by-night operations, not the by-products of established neighborhood life. Everyone is on their way somewhere, and as everyone needs somewhere to park their belongings, their kids or their parents, their documents or their dreams, Citayam is in one sense a big parking lot for vehicles that hardly can move. The station is the public, and its deliberations are all over the place as its constituencies head to and from many places.

Spatial configurations and the etching out of discernible territories are much less important than the rhythmic modulations of movement. Of course, it is important to find a place to identify in some way as "home," but finding the right rhythms of circulation, circumvention and interaction is the key to actually finding places to "live," to generate livelihood. In a city where more and more people do not stay at home, finding a strategic place to stay is a matter of rhythm. Governing here is a matter of residents finding the means to keep the flow going, of knowing how to improvise when itineraries are inevitably interrupted, of making the most of the detours and downtime, of converting downtime into opportunities to interact with unknown others, where there are no obligations, no promises of reciprocity, and where no one is likely to find out or judge you for any impulsive risks that you might undertake.

Many may have initially sought out Citayam as the realization of the imperative to become truly middle class and to escape labor-intensive residencies in popular neighborhoods of the urban core. But in the end, most cannot set themselves off definitively from a swirling "dialogue" with discrepant stories of implantation. They soon discover that this periphery is impervious to long-term horizons, and they eventually come to "work" the train line as a means of spawning idiosyncratic circulations through the larger region and across a tentative network of boarding house rooms, extra jobs, opportunities for their kids, and small investments here and there using the entire region as a canvas and these constantly re-inscribed itineraries as their "real home." It is dizzying to try to figure out how these multiple itineraries, circuits and weak intersections operate in any kind of concert, or to even follow the circuits of a single household, let alone those pursued by residents nominally living in the same district – now something whose borders and working definition are more diffuse than ever.

Despite the massive expropriation of funds from working-class mortgage payments for what would become uninhabitable districts, peripheries demonstrate themselves as something more than dumping grounds and yet it is not clear to what extent they offer themselves as a specific political ground. Rather in Citayam, the politics may be more about how to ensure residents continue to get to the train, about how to entrain the energies generated in this process to consolidate infrastructure and urban services in a way that is capable of following all the twists and turns of both the material and emerging social landscape without straightening out its vistas and contiguities of disparate functions (Amin and Thrift 2016). It entails not tying down residents to endless struggles to secure their albeit provisional positions, to locate security in maintaining the relative opacity of complexly woven environs that ward off big-time consolidations of land. It means retaining the periphery of the periphery as a source of food and improvised marketing systems that keep costs down. It means engaging the makeshift deliberations that residents in overly congested material and affective spaces conduct in order to accord each other some "right of way," some space of operation as a form of care. It means seeing care in the way in which holes are made in all of the enclosures that mark a particular propertied settlement and to see these apertures as forms of care.

It means looking at how the very intensity of segregating forces, of expulsions, land-grabs, and gentrification – which, indeed, are the predominant descriptors of contemporary urban development – also rebound in weird ways, suggesting, even for a moment, not the romance with urban cosmopolitan mixture, but a contingent density of differences that don't seem to know how to narrate how they all got to be in the same "neighborhood" (Hardt and Negri 2017). Big money may prevail, as well as grand schemes of self-contained, gated, and homogeneous lifestyles that offer prospective residents direct contact with a global world. But the underside of all of the compromises and adaptations necessary to pull off these "being part of the real world" projects reflects a plurality of small refusals, "switchbacks," rapid ascendancies and declines, where all kinds of apparent strangers end up having to catch "the same train."

It is a matter of attempting to walk the tightrope between refusing incorporation into the orders of power that render residents peripheral, that force them to the peripheries, and the attempts to appropriate the energies and creative manifestations of residents at the periphery by those same orders as a means of withdrawing from any responsibility to democratically govern (Gago 2015; Kanngieser and Beuret 2017). This navigation of the tightrope, however, does not have a single figure of resolution. It is an incessant tension, for that tension is the rhythm of practices that seem to neither refuse nor comply. As Barber points out (2017), "Politics is the problem that being cannot solve, and that is denied by the participation in and transit toward resolution. What is the essence of politics? It is not intervention in the distribution of being for the alternative possibilities of being; it is rather insistence on a no that 'precedes' – that antecedes, that is autonomous from – the transitivity to/ of being."

Segregation is real, but in city after city it is also replete with leaks, as both high-end and low-end constructions often fail to keep out the "elements" or are haunted by debilitating spirits, mountains of debt, or stifling boredom. Even when consuming classes express satisfaction and relief from having escaped the messy business of the old urban fabric, their anxieties about being "good enough subjects" exert their own wear and tear on all available sociality. A vast majority of residents are pharmaceutically inclined, accentuating a wavering line between exorbitant generosity and paranoia. Still an urban sensorium can't be weighed down by interminable calculations. Political decisions are seldom results of sustained deliberation but determinations to cut off recursive thought – religious, rational, or algorithmic – at the pass. Exposures are raw and unfiltered. The prevailing affective climate might lead one to conclude that most residents are ensconced behind closed doors. But the makeshift cafés, bars, and restaurants of Citayam, Les Eucalyptus, Abobo (Abidjan), and La Liberdad (Salvador Bahia) are full of tables covered with maps, notes, calls for proposals, and plots.

In a game of state politics, where affordances and territory are continuously reapportioned to different factions, where the overconfidence of big developers and real estate financiers is increasingly punctuated by an incessant anxiety of getting the timing right, of having to preside over intricate sutures of money, land, labor, technology, rules, and political deals, maintaining peripheries as spaces of compressed livelihoods, maneuvers, and backgrounds is critical. They not only offer a possible hedge against the bulldozing regimens of homogenizing shopping malls, industrial parks, and export-processing zones, but also are instruments of leverage within that very game.

Citayam offers a continuous stream of small refusals to be the henchman on the ground for this political game – a game funded by availing state authority, capital budgets, and implicit subsidies to real estate-generated accumulation. Municipal authorities, as far as they clearly exist in Citayam, constantly play the ambiguities of countervailing laws and policies regarding land disposition to fold in heterogeneous "projects" rather than offer large chunks of land to upscale consolidations. Long-standing agricultural families sublease land for multiple functions, each function acting as a possible multiplier effect of the other and a brake on expansionism by any one party. Tenants of new cheap housing built by "hit and run" developers quickly decide to forgo getting stuck with quickly deteriorated houses and make their own under-the-table deals to put facts on the ground by forming their own companies to develop small multi-level townhouses and stores co-financed by tertiary institutions looking to open new branches. It is a world of "strange alliances" that often fall apart in a matter of days, leaving their own residues of defeat. But they take place within an overarching atmosphere where the fear of failure is not dominant, does not impede initiatives to keep on trying things.

Urban life, no matter how configured and no matter the promises of automated efficiencies, remains labor-intensive. While residents in places like Citayam have often demonstrated their willingness to descend on the street, to participate in long, drawn-out battles for small wins, it is unreasonable to expect a politics of sustained antagonisms at the barricades. Just as they take what the periphery has to offer, which is largely a single train line and an overly congested terminus that branches out in intensifying fragmented lines of connection and coherence, we, too, should be able to take what they offer as a political practice, as a series of rhythms that enable surprising, frustrating, sometimes confusing, sentiments and practices of residents caring for and enduring with each other.

References

Aalbers, Manuel. 2011. The Revanchist Renewal of Yesterday's City of Tomorrow. *Antipode* 43: 1696–724.

Amin, Ash. 2014. Lively Infrastructure. *Theory, Culture and Society* 31: 137–61.

Amin, Ash. 2016. On Urban Failure. *Social Research: An International Journal* 83: 777–98.

Amin, Ash, and Nigel Thrift. 2016. *Seeing like a City*. London: Polity.

Amoore, Louise. 2006. Biometric Borders: Governing Mobilities in the War on Terror. *Political Geography* 25: 336–51.

Amoore, Louise. 2018. Cloud Geographies: Computing, Data, Sovereignty. *Progress in Human Geography* 42: 4–24.

Amoore, Louise, and Volha Piotukh. 2015. Life beyond Big Data: Governing with Little Analytics. *Economy and Society* 44: 341–66.

Anderson, Ben. 2017. Emergency Futures: Exception, Urgency, Interval, Hope. *Sociological Review* 65: 463–77.

Barber, Daniel Colucciello. 2016. The Creation of Non-Being. *Rhizomes: Cultural Studies in Emerging Knowledge* 29: https://doi.org/10.20415/rhiz/029.e10

Barber, Daniel Colucciello. 2017. Assembling No: Remarks on Diaspora and Intransitivity. *SubStance* 46: 155–65.

Bayat, Asef. 2015. Plebeians of the Arab Spring. *Current Anthropology* 56, S11: S33–43.

Bear, Laura. 2015. *Navigating Austerity: Currents of Debt along a South Asian River*. Stanford, CA: Stanford University Press.

Benjamin, Solomon. 2005. Touts, Pirates and Ghosts. *Sarai Reader: Bare Acts*. Delhi: Sarai, pp. 242–54.

Bhan, Gautam. 2016. *In the Public's Interest: Evictions, Citizenship and Inequality in Contemporary Delhi*. New Delhi: Orient Blackswan.

Bishop, Ryan. 2015. Smart Dust and Remote Sensing: The Political Subject in Autonomous Systems. *Cultural Politics* 11: 100–11.

Boyer, Dominic. 2017. Revolutionary Infrastructure. In Penny Harvey, Casper Bruun Jensen, and Atsuro Morita (eds.) *Infrastructures and Social Complexity: A Companion*. London: Routledge, pp. 174–86.

Bratton, Benjamin. 2016. *The Stack: On Software and Sovereignty*. Cambridge, MA: MIT Press.

Brenner, Neil. 2013. Theses on Urbanization. *Public Culture* 25: 85–114.

Brenner, Neil, and Christian Schmid. 2014. The "Urban Age" in Question. *International Journal of Urban and Regional Research* 38: 731–55.

Bryan, Dick, Michael Rafferty, and Chris Jefferis. 2015. Risk and Value: Finance, Labor, and Production. *South Atlantic Quarterly* 114: 307–29.

Caldeira, Teresa. 2016. Peripheral Urbanization: Autoconstruction, Transversal Logics, and Politics in Cities of the Global South. *Environment and Planning D: Society and Space* 35: 3–20.

Camacho, Marcos. 2017. There Is a Third Thing. *Hostis Journal*, July 22, 2017. Available at: http://incivility.org/?p=280.

Campt, Tina. 2012. *Image Matters: Archive, Photography, and the African Diaspora in Europe*. Durham, NC: Duke University Press.

Cohen, Tom, and Claire Colebrook. 2017. Vortices: On "Critical Climate Change" as a Project. *South Atlantic Quarterly* 116: 129–43.

Colebrook, Claire. 2014. *Death of the PostHuman: Essays on Extinction*, Vol. 1. Ann Arbor, MI: Open Humanities Press.

Colebrook, Claire. 2017. Sex and the (Anthropocene) City. *Theory, Culture and Society* 34: 39–60.

Corsín Jiménez, Alberto. 2008. Well-Being in Anthropological Balance: Remarks on Proportionality as Political Imagination. In Alberto Corsin-Jiminez (ed.) *Culture and Well-Being: Anthropological Approaches to Freedom and Political Ethics*. London: Pluto Press, pp. 180–97.

Corsín Jiménez, Alberto. 2017. Auto-construction Redux: The City as Method. *Cultural Anthropology* 42: 450–78.

Corsín Jiménez, Alberto, and Adolfo Estalella. 2013. The Atmospheric Person: Value, Experiment, and "Making Neighbors" in Madrid's Popular Assemblies. *Hau: Journal of Ethnographic Theory* 3: 119–39.

Crandall, Jordan. 2010. The Geospatialization of Calculative Operations: Tracking, Sensing, and Megacities. *Theory, Culture & Society* 27: 68–90.

Deleuze, Gilles. 1994. *Difference and Repetition*. New York: Columbia University Press.

Easterling, Keller. 2016. Histories of Things that Don't Happen and Shouldn't Always Work. *Social Research: An International Quarterly* 83: 626–44.

Elden, Stuart. 2010. Land, Terrain, Territory. *Progress in Human Geography* 34: 799–817.

Elden, Stuart. 2013. Secure the Volume: Vertical Geopolitics and the Depth of Power. *Political Geography* 34: 35–51.

Eshun, Kodowo. 1998. *More Brilliant than the Sun: Adventures in Sonic Fiction*. London: Quartet Books.

Esposito, Elena. 2013. The Structures of Uncertainty: Performativity and Unpredictability in Economic Operations. *Economy and Society* 42: 102–29.

Esposito, Elena. 2016. The Construction of Unpredictability. In Armen Avanessian and Suhail Malik (eds.) *The Time*

References

Complex: Post-Contemporary. Miami, FL: [Name], pp. 133–42.
Fanon, Frantz. 1967. *Black Skin, White Masks*. New York: Grove Press.
Fignolé, Jean-Claude. 1987. *Les Possédés de la pleine lune*. Paris: Editions du Seuil.
Gabrys, Jennifer. 2014. Programming Environments: Environmentality and Citizen Sensing in the Smart City. *Environment and Planning D: Society and Space* 32: 30–48.
Gabrys, Jennifer. 2017. Citizen Sensing, Air Pollution and Fracking: From "Caring about Your Air" to Speculative Practices of Evidencing Harm. *Sociological Review* 65: 172–92.
Gago, Verónica. 2015. Financialization of Popular Life and the Extractive Operations of Capital: A Perspective from Argentina. *South Atlantic Quarterly* 114: 11–28.
Galloway, Alexander. 2014. *Laruelle: Against the Digital*. Minneapolis, MN: University of Minnesota Press.
Galloway, Alexander, and Jason R. LaRivière. 2017. Compression in Philosophy. *Boundary2* 44: 125–47.
Gayer, Laurent, and Christophe Jaffrelot. 2012. *Muslims in Indian Cities: Trajectories of Marginalization*. London: Hurst.
Gerlitz, Carolin, and Celia Lury. 2014. Social Media and Self-Evaluating Assemblages: On Numbers, Orderings, and Values. *Distinktion: A Journal of Social Theory* 15: 174–88.
Ghertner, D. Asher. 2017. When Is the State? Topology, Temporality, and the Navigation of Everyday State Space in Delhi. *Annals of the American Association of Geographers* 107: 131–50.
Gidwani, Vinay, and Anant Maringanti. 2016. The Waste–Value Dialectic: Lumpen Urbanization in Contemporary India. *Comparative Studies of South Asia, Africa and the Middle East* 36: 112–33.
Glover, Kaiama. 2010. *Haiti Unbound: A Spiralist Challenge to the Postcolonial Canon*. Liverpool: Liverpool University Press.

Guironnet, Antoine, and Ludovic Halbert. 2014. The Financialization of Urban Development Projects: Concepts, Processes, and Implications. LATTS Working Paper hal-01097192 n14-04.

Hall, Suzanne, and Mike Savage. 2015. Animating the Urban Vortex: New Sociological Urgencies. *International Journal of Urban and Regional Research* 40: 82–95.

Hardt, Michael, and Antonio Negri. 2008. *Commonwealth*. Cambridge, MA: Harvard University Press.

Hardt, Michael, and Antonio Negri. 2017. *Assembly*. New York: Oxford University Press.

Harvey, David. 1989. *The Urban Experience*. Baltimore, MD: Johns Hopkins University Press.

Harvey, David. 2012. *Rebel Cities: From the Right to the City to the Urban Revolution*. London: Verso.

Holston, James. 1991. Autoconstruction in Working-Class Brazil. *Cultural Anthropology* 6: 447–65.

Hui, Yuk. 2016a. *On the Existence of Digital Objects*. Minneapolis, MN: University of Minnesota Press.

Hui, Yuk. 2016b. *The Question concerning Technology in China: An Essay in Cosmotechnics*. Windsor Quarry, UK: Urbanomics.

Jamia Millia Islamia. 2015. Baseline Survey of North-East District, NCT Delhi Minority Concentrated Districts Project, Ministry of Minority Affairs, Government of India.

Jamil, Ghazala. 2014. The Capitalist Logic of Spatial Segregation: A Study of Muslims in Delhi. *Economic and Political Weekly* 49: 52–8.

Jensen, Casper Bruun. 2015. Experimenting with Political Materials: Environmental Infrastructure and Ontological Transformations. *Distinktion: Journal of Social Theory* 16: 17–30.

Kanngieser, Anja, and Nicholas Beuret. 2017. Refusing the World: Silence, Commoning, and the Anthropocene. *South Atlantic Quarterly* 116: 363–80.

Keil, Roger. 2017. *Suburban Planet: Making the Urban World from the Outside In*. Cambridge: Polity.

Kitchin, Rob. 2014. The Real-Time City? Big Data and Smart Urbanism. *Geojournal* 79: 1–14.

Larkin, Brian. 2013. The Politics and Poetics on Infrastructure. *Annual Review of Anthropology* 42: 327–43.

Laruelle, François. 1999. A Summary of Non-Philosophy. *Pli* 8: 138–48.

Laruelle, François. 2011. The Generic as Predicate and Constant: Non-Philosophy and Materialism. In Lev Bryant, Nick Srnicek and Graham Harman (eds.) *The Speculative Turn: Continental Materialism and Realism.* Melbourne: re.press, pp. 237–60.

Leszczynski, Agnes. 2016. Speculative Futures: Cities, Data, and Governance beyond Smart Urbanism. *Environment and Planning A* 48: 1691–708.

Lingis, Alphonso. 1994. *The Community of Those who Have Nothing in Common.* Bloomington, IN: University of Indiana Press.

Luque-Ayala, Andres, and Simon Marvin. 2015. The Maintenance of Urban Circulation: An Operational Logic of Infrastructural Control. *Environment and Planning D: Society and Space* 34: 91–108.

Lury, Celia. 2018. Shifters as Figures of Speech: "Not in Our Name" and "Je suis Charlie" (unpublished).

MacKenzie, Adrian. 2015. Digital Sociology in the Field of Devices. In Laurie Hanquinet and Mike Savage (eds.) *Routledge International Handbook of Sociology of Art and Culture.* London: Routledge.

Marriot, David. 2016. Judging Fanon. *Rhizomes: Cultural Studies in Emerging Knowledge* 29: https://doi.org/10.20415/rhiz/029.e03

Martin, Randy. 2013. After Economy? Social Logics of the Derivative. *Social Text* 114: 83–106.

Martin, Randy. 2015. *Knowledge LTD: Towards a Social Logic of the Derivative.* Philadelphia, PA: Temple University Press.

Mbembe, Achille. 2017. *Critique of Black Reason.* Durham, NC: Duke University Press.

McFarlane, Colin. 2016. The Geographies of Urban Density: Topology, Politics and the City. *Progress in Human Geography* 40: 629–48.

McKittrick, Katherine. 2013. Plantation Futures. *Small Axe: A Caribbean Platform for Criticism* 17: 1–15.

McKittrick, Katherine. 2016. Rebellion/Invention/Groove. *Small Axe: A Caribbean Platform for Criticism* 20: 79–91.

McKittrick, Katherine, and Alex Weheliye. 2017. 808s & Heartbreak. *Propter Nos* 2: 13–42.

Mezzadra, Sandro, and Brett Neilson. 2012. Between Inclusion and Exclusion: On the Topology of Global Space and Borders. *Theory, Culture & Society* 29: 58–75.

Mezzadra, Sandro, and Brett Neilson. 2015. Operations of Capital. *South Atlantic Quarterly* 114: 1–9.

Morrison, Toni. 2012. *Home*. New York: Alfred A. Knopf.

Moten, Fred. 2008. The Case of Blackness. *Criticism* 50: 177–218.

Moten, Fred. 2017. *Black and Blur*. Durham, NC: Duke University Press.

Muniesa, Fabian. 2014. *The Provoked Economy: Economic Reality and the Performative Turn*. London: Routledge.

Neyrat, Frédéric. 2016. Planetary Antigones: The Environmental Situation and the Wandering Condition. *Qui Parle* 25: 35–64.

Parisi, Luciana. 2013. *Contagious Architecture: Computation, Aesthetics and Space*. Cambridge, MA: MIT Press.

Parks, Lisa. 2016. Drones, Vertical Mediation, and the Targeted Class. *Feminist Studies* 42: 227–35.

Pine, Jason. 2012. *The Art of Making Do in Naples*. Minneapolis, MN: University of Minnesota Press.

Povinelli, Elizabeth. 2017. The Ends of Humans: Anthropocene, Autonomism, Antagonism, and the Illusions of Our Epoch. *South Atlantic Quarterly* 116: 293–310.

Puig de la Bellacasa, Maria. 2011. Matters of Care in Technoscience: Assembling Neglected Things. *Social Studies of Science* 41: 85–106.

Raengo, Alessandra. 2016. Black Matters. *Discourse* 38: 246–64.

Riles, Annelise. 2010. Collateral Expertise. *Current Anthropology* 51: 795–818.

Roberts, Elizabeth F. S. 2017. What Gets Inside: Violent Entanglements and Toxic Boundaries in Mexico City. *Cultural Anthropology* 32: 592–619.

Robinson, Jennifer. 2016. Thinking Cities through Elsewhere: Comparative Tactics for a More Global Urban Studies. *Progress in Human Geography* 40: 3–29.

Rouanet, Hortense, and Ludovic Halbert. 2016. Leveraging Finance Capital: Urban Change and Self-Empowerment of Real Estate Developers in India. *Urban Studies* 53: 1401–23.

Ruddick, Sue. 2015. Situating the Anthropocene: Planetary Urbanization and the Anthropological Machine. *Urban Geography* 36: 1113–30.

Sassen, Saskia. 2010. When the City Itself Becomes a Technology of War. *Theory, Culture and Society* 27: 33–50.

Satia, Prya. 2014. Drones: A History from the British Middle East. *Humanity* 5: 1–31.

Sevilla-Buitrago, Alvaro. 2015. Capitalist Formations of Enclosure: Space and the Extinction of the Commons. *Antipode* 47: 999–1020.

Sites, William. 2012. Radical Culture in Black Necropolis: Sun Ra, Alton Abraham and Postwar Chicago. *Journal of Urban History* 38: 687–719.

Srivastava, Sanjay. 2014. *Entangled Urbanism: Slum, Gated Community and Shopping Mall in Delhi and Gurgaon.* New York: Oxford University Press.

Stephenson, Niamh, and Dimitris Papadopoulos. 2006. Outside Politics/Continuous Experience. *Ephemera: Theory and Politics in Organization* 6: 433–53.

Stiegler, Bernard. 2010. *For a Critique of Political Economy.* Cambridge: Polity.

Stiegler, Bernard. 2016. *Automatic Society*, Vol. 1: *The Future of Work.* Cambridge: Polity.

Stoler, Ann Louise. 2016. *Duress: Imperial Durabilities in Our Times.* Durham, NC: Duke University Press.

Tarlo, Emma. 2001. Welcome to History: A Resettlement Colony in the Making. In Emma Tarlo, Veronique Dupont, and Denis Vidal (eds.) *Delhi: Urban Space and Human Destinies.* Delhi: Manohar.

Thrift, Nigel. 2012. The Insubstantial Pageant: Producing an Untoward Land. *Cultural Geographies* 19: 141–68.

Tsing, Anna Lowenhaupt. 2012. On Nonscalability: The Living World Is Not Amenable to Precision-Nested Scales. *Common Knowledge* 18: 505–24.

Tsing, Anna Lowenhaupt. 2013. Sorting Out Commodities: How Capitalist Value Is Made through Gifts. *Hau: Journal of Ethnographic Theory* 3: 21–43.

Viveiros de Castro, Eduardo. 2014. *Cannibal Metaphysics*. Minneapolis, MN: University of Minnesota Press.

Wagner, Roy. 2011. 'Vújà De and the Quintessentialists' Guild. *Common Knowledge* 17: 155–62.

Wills, David. 2016. *Inanimation: Theories of Inorganic Life*. Minneapolis, MN: University of Minnesota Press.

Wyly, Elvin. 2015. Gentrification on the Planetary Urban Frontier: Turner's Noösphere. *Urban Studies* 52: 2515–50.

Index

Index

Index

Index

Index

Voice of Islam, 104–6

Weheliye, Alex, 92
welfare associations, 77–8, 84
WhatsApp groups, 79–80

William, Eduardo, 7–9

YouTube, 18

Zionism, 116